DATE DUE

DATE DUE			
NO 2 '62			
NO 16 '62			
MY 21 '63			
MA 21 '64			
MR 25 '66			
NO 29 '66			
DE 12 '67			
MR 26 '68			
NO 7 '72			
NO 14 '72			
NOV 20 1972			
JUN 0 3 1977			
SEP AX 01 1972			
MAY 0 6 2013			
APR 2 2 2013			
GAYLORD			PRINTED IN U.S.A

RHYMES AND VERSES

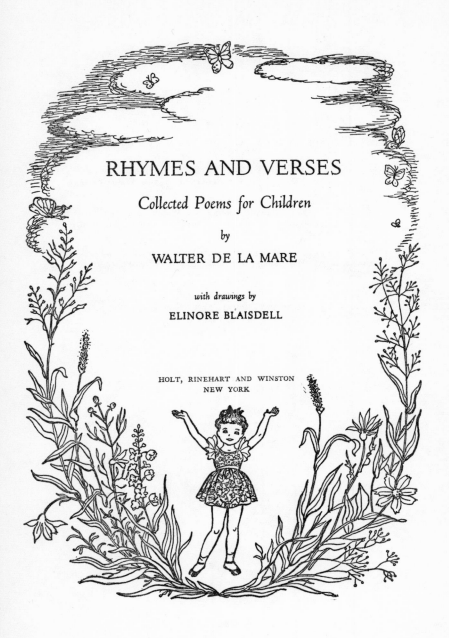

RHYMES AND VERSES

Collected Poems for Children

by

WALTER DE LA MARE

with drawings by

ELINORE BLAISDELL

HOLT, RINEHART AND WINSTON
NEW YORK

Published, February, 1947
Second Printing, April, 1957
Third Printing, October, 1958
Fourth Printing, September, 1961

91798-0217

PRINTED IN THE UNITED STATES OF AMERICA

CONTENTS

GREEN GROW THE RASHES, O!

ALL ROUND ABOUT THE TOWN

[v]

[vi]

FAIRIES — WITCHES — PHANTOMS

WINTER AND CHRISTMAS

BOOKS AND STORIES

MOON AND STARS — NIGHT AND DREAM

ODDS AND ENDS

[xi]

ACKNOWLEDGMENTS

Acknowledgment is made for permission to include the poems from the following collections:

BELLS AND GRASS, published by Viking Press, Inc.

COME HITHER, published by Alfred A. Knopf, Inc.

CROSSINGS, published by Alfred A. Knopf, Inc.

DOWN-ADOWN-DERRY, published by Henry Holt and Company, Inc.

FLORA, published by William Heinemann, Ltd. and J. B. Lippincott Company

PEACOCK PIE, published by Henry Holt and Company, Inc.

POEMS, published by Henry Holt and Company, Inc.

SONGS OF CHILDHOOD, published by Henry Holt and Company, Inc.

STUFF AND NONSENSE, published by Henry Holt and Company, Inc.

THIS YEAR: NEXT YEAR, published by Henry Holt and Company, Inc.

THE THREE ROYAL MONKEYS, published by Faber & Faber

Green Grow
The Rashes, O!

FOL DOL DO

Fol, dol, do, and a south wind a-blowing O,
Fol, dol, do, and green growths a-growing O,
Fol, dol, do, and the heart inside me knowing O,
    'Tis merry merry month of May.

Fol, dol, do, shrill chanticlere's a-crowing O,
Fol, dol, do, and the mower's soon a-mowing O,
O lovelier than the lilac tree, my lovely love's a-showing O,
    In merry merry month of May.

DAYBREAK

After the dark of night
Spreads slowly up the glow
Into the starry height
Of daybreak piercing through.

Now 'gin the cocks to crow;
Runs lapwing, claw and crest;
From her green haunt the hare
Lopes wet with dew. The east

Gathers its cloudy host
Into its soundless pen;
Stirring in their warm sleep,
Beasts rise and graze again.

Now, with his face on fire,
And drenched with sunbeams
   through
Sam, with his dappled team,
Drags out the iron plough.

Glistens with drops the grass;
Sighing, with joy, the trees
Stoop their green leafiness
Into the breeze.

Earth's wake now: every heart,
Wing, foot, and eye
Revels in light and heat:
The Sun's in the sky!

THE FOUR BROTHERS

Hithery, hethery — I love best
The wind that blows from out the West,
Breathing balm, and sweet of musk,
Rosy at morning, rosy at dusk.

Wind from the North, Oho, and Oho!
Climbs with his white mules laden with snow,
Up through the mirk plod muffled by
Master and mules through the louring sky.

Wind from the South lags back again
With bags of jewels from out of Spain;
A hole in the corner, and out they come —
May-bud, apple-bud, bramble-bloom.

Black runs the East, with clouted hair,
Grim as a spectre through the air,
And, with his lash, drives in again
Beasts to stall, to their fireside men.

FIVE OF US

" Five of us small merry ones,
And Simon in the grass.
Here's an hour for delight,
Out of mortal thought and sight.
See, the sunshine ebbs away:
We play and we play.

" Five of us small merry ones,
And yonder there the stone,
Flat and heavy, dark and cold,
Where, beneath the churchyard
  mould,

Time has buried yesterday:
We play and we play.

" Five of us small merry ones,
We sang a dirge, did we,
Cloud was cold on foot and hair,
And a magpie from her lair
Spread her motley in the air;
And we wept — our tears away:
We play and we play."

THE RAINBOW

I saw the lovely arch
Of Rainbow span the sky,
The gold sun burning
As the rain swept by.

In bright-ringed solitude
The showery foliage shone
One lovely moment,
And the Bow was gone.

THE GARDEN
(*For a Picture*)

That wooden hive between the trees
Is Palace of a Queen — of Bees.
With seed-black eyes, and hidden stings,
Sentries, at entry, beat their wings
To cool the night-dark gallery
Where waxen-celled Princesses lie;
And drones — their grubs — sleep snug near by,
    While busier bees store honey.

From the bright flowers in the bed —
    Ripening pippins overhead —
Some pollen cull to kneed bee-bread,
Or nectar still — for life and love,
    Love on both sides, not money.

Soon the two doves in the pale green grass
    With whirr of wing
    Will airward spring
And perch upon the table;
    Then tapping beaks
    Will peck the cakes,
And nibble, nibble, nibble;
For no-one's peering from the door
    Or peeping from the gable.

THE HUNT

Tallyho! Tallyho! —
Echo faints far astray,
On the still, misty air,
And the Hunt is away!
Horsemen and hounds
Stream over the hill;

And, brush well behind him,
Pelts with a will
Old Reynard the Fox —
As in conscience he may,
For hot at his heels
Sweep Trim, Trap and Tray;

Chestnut, and black,
And flea-bitten grey.
But the Crafty One knows
Every inch of the way!
Thicket and spinney,
Gully and dell,
Where the stream runs deep,
And the otters dwell —
Hemlock, garlic,
Bog asphodel —
He'll lead them a dance,
Though they ride like hell.
And — wily old animal,
Cunning as they! —
He'll live — to go hunting —
Another fine day.

OFF THE GROUND

Three jolly Farmers
Once bet a pound
Each dance the others would
Off the ground.
Out of their coats
They slipped right soon,
And neat and nicesome,
Put each his shoon.

One — Two — Three! —
And away they go,
Not too fast,
And not too slow;
Out from the elm-tree's
Noonday shadow,
Into the sun
And across the meadow.
Past the schoolroom,

With knees well bent,
Fingers a-flicking,
They dancing went.
Upsides and over,
And round and round,
They crossed click-clacking,
The Parish bound.
By Tupman's meadow
They did their mile,
Tee-to-tum
On a three-barred stile.
Then straight through
    Whipham,
Downhill to Week,
Footing it lightsome,
But not too quick,
Up fields to Watchet,
And on through Wye,

Till seven fine churches
They'd seen skip by —
Seven fine churches,
And five old mills,
Farms in the valley,
And sheep on the hills;
Old Man's Acre
And Dead Man's Pool
All left behind,
As they danced through Wool.

And Wool gone by,
Like tops that seem
To spin in sleep
They danced in dream:
Withy — Wellover —
Wassop — Wo —
Like an old clock
Their heels did go.
A league and a league
And a league they went,
And not one weary,
And not one spent.
And lo, and behold!
Past Willow-cum-Leigh
Stretched with its waters
The great green sea.

Says Farmer Bates,
" I puffs and I blows,
What's under the water,
Why, no man knows! "
Says Farmer Giles,
" My wind comes weak,
And a good man drownded
Is far to seek."
But Farmer Turvey,
On twirling toes

Up's with his gaiters,
And in he goes:
Down where the mermaids
Pluck and play
On their twangling harps
In a sea-green day;
Down where the mermaids,
Finned and fair,
Sleek with their combs
Their yellow hair. . . .

Bates and Giles —
On the shingle sat,
Gazing at Turvey's
Floating hat.
But never a ripple
Nor bubble told
Where he was supping
Off plates of gold.
Never an echo
Rilled through the sea
Of the feasting and dancing
And minstrelsy.
They called — called — called:
Came no reply:
Nought but the ripples'
Sandy sigh.
Then glum and silent
They sat instead,
Vacantly brooding
On home and bed,
Till both together
Stood up and said: —
" Us knows not, dreams not,
Where you be,
Turvey, unless
In the deep blue sea;
But axcusing silver —

And it comes most willing —
Here's us two paying
Our forty shilling;
For it's sartin sure, Turvey,
Safe and sound,
You danced us square, Turvey;
Off the ground! "

BUNCHES OF GRAPES

" Bunches of grapes," says Timothy;
" Pomegranates pink," says Elaine;
" A junket of cream and a cranberry tart
    For me," says Jane.

" Love-in-a-mist," says Timothy;
" Primroses pale," says Elaine;
" A nosegay of pinks and mignonette
    For me," says Jane.

" Chariots of gold," says Timothy;
" Silvery wings," says Elaine;
" A bumpity ride in a wagon of hay
    For me," says Jane.

SALLIE

When Sallie with her pitcher goes
Down the long lane where the hawthorn blows
    For water from the spring,
I watch her bobbing sun-bright hair,
In the green leaves and blossoms there,
Shining and gleaming primrose-fair;
Till back again, like bird on wing,
Her pitcher, brimmed, she turns to bring —
    Oh, what a joy to see!
And her clear voice, the birds' above,
Rings sweet with joy, entranced with love —
    Ah! would 'twere love for me!

NICOLETTA

Oh, my pretty Nicoletta,
Come away, come away!
There's a linnet in the willow,
And the moon is up today,
When the one is sleepy silent
And the other wildly clear,
I know a hazel thicket
Where I'll kiss you, dear.

Ah, sweetheart Nicoletta,
Come away, come away!
There are rabbits in the warren,
There is blossom on the may;
And when the first are nibbling
And the other's cold with dew,
I'll tell you tales of magic,
And of moonshine, and of you.

Come away, Nicoletta,
Nicoletta-likkalay!
There's a secret I must sigh you
And a hidden thing to say;
Creep out as soon as evening comes,
Not a wink your eyelids close,
And I'll show you where on hills of dream
The wild thyme blows.

MARY

Mary! Mary! *Mary!*
Come to the dairy, please!
Give me some butter to spread on my bread,
Give me a morsel of cheese.
The cows in the meadow are chewing the cud,
Some of them deep in the stream —

Give me a suppet of curds and whey,
Or a wee little bowl of cream!
It's half a week since breakfast,
And cook won't spare a crumb;
Fol-di-diddle-O, starve I shall,
Unless, you dear, you come!
A hungry wolf's inside me,
Though I wouldn't for worlds just tease:
Mary! Mary! *Mary!*
Come to the dairy, *please!*

THUNDER

Call the cows home!
Call the cows home!
Louring storm clouds
Hitherward come;
East to West
Their wings are spread;
Lost in the blue
Is each heaven-high head;
They've dimmed the sun;
Turned day to night;
With a whistling wind
The woods are white;
Down streams the rain
On farm, barn, byre,
Bright green hill,
And bramble and brier,
Filling the valley
With glimmer and gloom:
Call the cows home!
Call the cows home!

THE SHEPHERD

When I was out one morning —
In a meadow, white with sheep,
Lay a shepherd by a haystack
    Fast asleep.

With me the lark was carolling,
There was gold and green and blue;
But what, you drowsy shepherd,
    Was with you?

Was it night and water gushing
And moonbeams cold and clear
On the softly silver-slipping
    Dripping weir?

Was it childhood, was it sweetheart,
Was it distant isles and seas,
Day of Judgment, Harvest Home, or
    Bread and cheese?

HIGH

    Fly, kite!
    High!
    Till you touch the sky!
  Stoop, whistling in the wind;
And whisper down the quivering string
    If, as you soar, you find
The world we tread is like a ball —
With mounds for hills, and ponds for seas,
Its oxen small as creeping bees,
    Mere bushes its huge trees!
But ah, the dew begins to fall,
    The evening star to shine,
Down you must sink to earth again —
    An earth, I mean, like mine.

AWAY WE GO

One, two, three,
And away go we!
Shingle, starfish,
Sand, and sea!
Wind on cheek,
Clear sun on skin;
The tumbling waves
Sweep out, sweep in.

A magic, broken
Music calls
In the water
As it falls;
Voices, a sigh,
A long-drawn *hush,*
As back — in myriad
Bubbles — gush
The green-grey ripples,
Flecked with snow —
A music solemn,
Sweet, and low.

MR. PUNCH
(*For a Picture*)

A screech across the sands;
    A drum's dull thump;
Oh, wicked Mr. Punch,
    Hook-nose and hump!
What corpse is this lies here? —
    An infant dear;
And Judy listening
    In grief and fear,
Knowing the Hangman
With his rope draws near!

[14]

While lean Dog Toby yawns —
          Ruff, paws, and tail —
And now at starfish blinks,
          And now at pail.
A screech across the sands!
          That sullen thump!
Oh, wicked Mr. Punch,
          Belled-cap, hook-nose and hump!

ALL THE FUN

(*For a Picture*)

Here's all the Fun of the Fair! Come buy!
Chute, and swing, and a penny a shy!
          And the lamps will blaze at night —
The dangling lamps that drip and hiss
Where peppermint, candy and liquorice,
Bull's-eyes, hardbake, coconut-ice,
          Are a farthing, or less, a bite.

The gilded organs blare and groan,
Jack rides the skewbald, Ruth the roan,
          Finger and knee clutched tight.
Giddily galloping on they course . . .
But who is it sits the little blue horse?
What stranger straddles that dark little horse,
          Half hidden out of sight?

And when, all silent, dark, and still
Are tent and tree-top, meadow and hill,
          Merry-go-round and man,
When the autumn stars shine faint above,
And the barn-owl hoots from her secret grove,
And the shades of night begin to rove,
I wonder what he'll be dreaming of —
          The gypsy-boy in the Van.

HARVEST

(For a Picture)

Poppy, cornflower, nid-nod wheat,
    The sheaves are ripe for rick.
And perched aloft in the dusty glow
    Toils on hot, red-faced Dick.
A sultry and enormous sun
    Sinks slowly in the West;
Another harvest day is done;
And soon — these humans homeward gone —
    The fields will be at rest.
Soon, when the moon shines honey-pale
    On the wide world's round breast,
Silv'ring the cherries of the dwale
    And that green woodland's crest,
These horses will in stable be,
    This silent bird in nest.

HOLIDAYS

(For a Picture)

Dobbin's in stable, pigs are in sty —
Norfolk Dumpling and Twinkle-eye —
    And milking time is come.
Four cows stand drowsing, head to tail,
Waiting for Moll with her stool and pail,
    And two are trotting home.
The sea lies flat as a pane of glass;
    Languid and faint the air,
The shadows lengthen in the grass —
    Was ever day so fair?
The wheat's in sheaf, a clucking hen
    Pecks supper for her chicks;
(And if not one is out of sight,
    She has precisely six).

[16]

The engine puffs, the people sit,
    And out of window gaze
At lank-legged Peggy with the switch
She cut at dawn — the switch with which
    She wooed her beasts to graze;
And (since he's hidden behind the cows)
They hear an unseen dog's bow-wows!

What wonder in a scene so bright
Their hearts are brimming with delight,
Welling with songs of joy and praise!
What wonder! Why, this very night
    Begins the Holidays!

HAYMAKING

    Bill's on the hay-wain
    Sam's below,
And Simon's up on the stack;
    Jeremy Joe
    Is behind — and so
He must be at the back!
    Tiny Tim,
    By the horse (that's him),
Gives him a wisp to munch;
    But Little Boy Blue
    We can't see you —
Snuggled asleep, maybe, under a wall,
Cows and sheep far out of call,
    Or eyeing what's there, for lunch.

NO BED

No bed! no bed! we shouted,
And wheeled our eyes from home
To where the green and golden woods
    Cried, Come!

Wild sang the evening birds,
The sun-clouds shone in our eyes,
A silver snippet of moon hung low
    In the skies.

We ran, we leapt, we sang,
We yodelled loud and shrill,
Chased Nobody through the valley and
    Up the hill.

We laughed, we quarrelled, we drank
The cool sweet of the dew,
Beading on bud and leaf the dim
    Woods through.

We stayed, we listened, we looked —
Now dark was on the prowl!
Too-whit-a-woo, from its hollow called
    An owl. . . .

O sleep, at last to slide
Into eyes made drunk with light;
Call in thy footsore boys to harmless
    Night!

WHERE

Houses! houses! — Oh, I know
Where the clovers are in blow;
Where the bee for nectar goes
From the clovers to the rose;
Where the rose that was a bud
Stands wide open in the wood;
Where the wood is thick with trees
Tossed to sunshine in the breeze;
Where the breezes whisper, " Come!
Listen, far one, here is home! "

All Round About the Town

THEN

Twenty, forty, sixty, eighty,
    A hundred years ago,
All through the night with lantern bright
    The Watch trudged to and fro.
And little boys tucked snug abed
    Would wake from dreams to hear —
" Two o' the morning by the clock,
    And the stars a-shining clear! "
Or, when across the chimney-tops
    Screamed shrill a North-East gale,
A faint and shaken voice would shout,
    " Three! — and a storm of hail! "

THE FIDDLERS

Nine feat Fiddlers had good Queen Bess
To play her music as she did dress.
Behind an arras of horse and hound
They sate there scraping delightsome sound.
Spangled, bejewelled, her skirts would she
Draw o'er a petticoat of cramasie;
And soft each string like a bird would sing
In the starry dusk of evening.
Then slow from the deeps the crisscross bows,
Crooning like doves, arose and arose.
When, like a cage, did her ladies raise
A stiff rich splendour o'er her ribbed stays,
Like bumbling bees those four times nine
Fingers in melodies loud did pine;
Last came her coif and her violet shoon
And her virgin face shone out like the moon:
Oh, then in a rapture those three times three
Fiddlers squealed shrill on their topmost C.

THERE SATE GOOD QUEEN BESS

There sate Good Queen Bess, oh,
A-shining on her throne.
Up, Jessie; down, docket;
My money's gone!

UP AND DOWN

Down the Hill of Ludgate,
Up the Hill of Fleet,
To and fro and East and West
With people flows the street;

Even the King of England
On Temple Bar must beat
For leave to ride to Ludgate
Down the Hill of Fleet.

DAYBREAK

The curtains of the solemn night
Draw back; and daybreak fair
Shines on these tulips cold with dew,
And fills with light the air.
No child stands tiptoe yet to sip
Clear water from the fountain's lip;
Nothing stirs anywhere,
But the birds in the dust, the leaves in the breeze
The nut-brown squirrels in the trees;
And empty is every chair.

THE WINDOW

Behind the blinds I sit and watch
The people passing—passing by;
And not a single one can see
My tiny watching eye.

They cannot see my little room,
All yellowed with the shaded sun,
They do not even know I'm here;
Nor'll guess when I am gone.

[24]

THE ROOM

(For a Picture)

Pot on the mantel; picture; clock —
A naked, marble Cupid — look!
    And, in the grate, a fire,
Whose wild bright flames in pallid smoke
    Branch higher yet, and higher:
A leather pouffe beside a chair,
    Its cushion striped with blue;
A pair of slippers on the kerb;
    And logs laid ready — two.
And see — a portrait hanging there,
    Dark hair, and darker eyes,
Above a pitcher filled with flowers
    Whose Springlike incense lies
In drifts of sweetness on the air —
    Proving the loved may find
That even when they are far from sight
    They are not out of mind.

NOT I!

As I came out of Wiseman's Street,
The air was thick with driven sleet;
Crossing over Proudman's Square
Cold louring clouds obscuring the air;
But as I entered Goodman's Lane
The burning sun came out again;
And on the roofs of Children's Row
In solemn glory shone the snow.

There did I lodge; there hope to die:
Envying no man — no, not I.

POOH!

Dainty Miss Apathy
Sat on a sofa,
Dangling her legs,
And with nothing to do;
She looked at a drawing of
Old Queen Victoria,
At a rug from far Persia —
An exquisite blue;
At a bowl of bright tulips;
A needlework picture
Of doves caged in wicker
You could almost hear coo;
She looked at the switch
That evokes e-
Lectricity;
At the coals of an age
B.C. millions and two —

When the trees were like ferns
And the reptiles all flew;
She looked at the cat
Asleep on the hearthrug,
At the sky at the window —
The clouds in it, too;
And a marvellous light
From the West burning
 through:
And the one silly word
In her desolate noodle
As she dangled her legs,
Having nothing to do,
Was not, as you'd guess,
Of dumbfoundered felicity,
But contained just four letters,
And these pronounced *POOH!*

WON'T

See, Master Proud-Face!
Cold as a stone;
Light, life, love
From his bright eyes gone;
Pale as a pudding
His smooth round cheek;
His head like a block
On his stiff, wooden neck.

Won't, says his cherry mouth;
Won't, says his chin;
Won't, says the Spectre,
His bosom within;
Won't, says his clenched fist;
Won't, says his foot;
Every single inch of him

Shouts, I will *NOT!* . . .

Poor, poor Mamma —
She mopes in her room,
Pining and pining
For the moment to come
When her short sharp you
    SHALL!
She can safely unsay,
And the sun sparkle out,
And the tears dry away;

Yes, her whole heart is sighing
In passionate trust
For a kiss from those *Won'ts*
To make hay of her Must!

THE DUNCE

Why does he still keep ticking?
    Why does his round white face
Stare at me over the books and ink,
    And mock at my disgrace?
Why does that thrush call, " Dunce, dunce, dunce! "?
    Why does that bluebottle buzz?
Why does the sun so silent shine? —
    And what do I care if it does?

SILLY SALLIE

Silly Sallie! Silly Sallie!
Called the boys down Blind Man's Alley;
But she, still smiling, never made
A sign she had heard, or answer gave;
Her blue eyes in her skimpy hair
Seemed not to notice they were there;
Seemed still to be watching, rain or shine,
Some other place, not out, but in:
Though it pleased the boys in Blind Man's Alley
Still to be shouting *Silly Sallie!*

BREAD AND CHERRIES

" Cherries, ripe cherries! "
    The old woman cried,
In her snowy white apron,
    And basket beside;

And the little boys came,
    Eyes shining, cheeks red,
To buy bags of cherries
    To eat with their bread.

I CAN'T ABEAR

I can't abear a Butcher,
    I can't abide his meat,
The ugliest shop of all is his,
    The ugliest in the street;
Bakers' are warm, cobblers' dark
    Chemists' burn watery lights;
But oh, the sawdust butcher's shop,
    That ugliest of sights!

ESMERALDA

(*For a Picture*)

Plump Mrs. Brown, we may suppose,
With basket and umbrella goes
Shopping. Why? Because she knows
That rain will pelt till dark comes down —
On wood and meadow; street and town;
That rain's set in till shut of day,
And the watery world is hidden away:
What use then still indoors to stay?

She sallies out with her small daughter:
These two young urchins following after,
Snailed in as snug as snug can be —
With rainy nose and blinking eye
Jack-boots, sou'wester, cap-à-pie —
Like sailors, in a gale at sea;
And aching fit to burst with laughter
At watching Mrs. Brown forget
Her Esmeralda's getting wet!

[29]

THE PENNY OWING

Poor blind Tam, the beggarman,
I'll give a penny to as soon as I can.
Where he stood at the corner in his rags, and cried,
The sun without shadow does now abide.

Safe be my penny till I come some day
To where Tam's waiting. And then I'll say,
" Here is my ghost, Tam, from the fire and dew,
And the penny I grudged kept safe for you."

THE BARBER'S

Gold locks, and black locks,
    Red locks, and brown,
Topknot to love-curl
    The hair wisps down;
Straight above the clear eyes,
    Rounded round the ears,
Snip-snap and snick-a-snick,
    Clash the Barber's shears;

Us, in the looking-glass,
    Footsteps in the street,
Over, under, to and fro,
    The lean blades meet;
Bay Rum or Bear's Grease,
    A silver groat to pay —
Then out a-shin-shan-shining
    In the bright, blue day.

COALS

In drowsy fit
I hear the flames
Syllabling o'er
Their ancient names:
The coals — a glory
Of gold — blaze on,

Drenched with the suns
Of centuries gone;
While, at the window,
This rainy day
In darkening twilight
Dies away.

[30]

THE CUPBOARD

I know a little cupboard,
With a teeny tiny key,
And there's a jar of Lollipops
    For me, me, me.

It has a little shelf, my dear,
As dark as dark can be,
And there's a dish of Banbury Cakes
    For me, me, me.

I have a small fat grandmamma,
With a very slippery knee,
And she's Keeper of the Cupboard,
    With the key, key, key.

And when I'm very good, my dear,
As good as good can be,
There's Banbury Cakes, and Lollipops
    For me, me, me.

THE LITTLE SHOP

(*For a Picture*)

The Whistler on the whistle
    Asks a penny — and is gone;
The scampering dog behind the lamp
    Hies off to thieve a bone;
"Williams & Sons" at Ninety-two
    Stay open — till they are shut,
Sell balls, bears, boxes, beads and barrows,
    Masks and fireworks — BUT: —

The *oldest* Shop, to the ends of the earth,
    Is in Little Old Nowhere Street;
Where rivers of Eden, named Now and Then,
    Sing, as their waters meet;

[31]

And the ribs of the coracle bleach in the sand
Wherein Nemo, the Sailorman, came to land.

Shem, Ham, Japheth, the wise declare,
    Found a booth where its bell now clinks;
The sun that gilded Absalom's hair
    Through its bottle-glass window blinks;
Here a child named Cæsar bought lumps of lead —
To melt and to mould into soldiers, he said.

An all-sorts shop; where Alfred tasted
    His first little sip of mead,
Five years, at least (a child of six),
    Before he was taught to read;
Hither came Stephen, hawk on wrist;
In its garden Prince Hal a sweetheart kissed.

A bottle of lollipops loved by Bess
    Stood apart on a window shelf.
When William, her poet, came in as a child,
    He smiled, and he helped himself;
And, munching at counter, carved his name
Where little Dan Chaucer had done the same.

Here Raleigh first peered at a Map of the World.
    And from over the snow on the wold
A wean, called Francis Bacon, came —
    Not a day over six years old,
So parched with the blast, he could scarcely speak:
" I want, so it please you, some books in Greek."

The two doomed children who asked for bread,
    Were given, alas, a stone.
Their uncle, whom folks called Crookback, had
    Sneaked in through the dusk — alone.
" Bird-lime," he mumbled. But Francis Drake
Bought marbles; and tackle, a ship to make.

A long-faced prince, not five foot tall,
      A Sceptre and Crown bespoke,
But the Crown his dark head failed to fit,
      And the golden Sceptre broke.
Another Prince Charlie, with ringleted hair,
Chose beads — for a lassie he loved to wear.

A huge black cat on the counter drowsed
      In the sunshine, hot through the glass,
Blinking his yellow eyes, narrow as slits,
      At the geese outside in the grass,
When he spied a boy, his face like a hawk's,
Who in for a penn'orth of powder stalks,
      And muttered, " My ' name '? 'Tis Fawkes."

Dolls, knives, string, and things to eat —
      Ginger-bread, buns, mince-pie,
Cram that bottle-glass window in Nowhere Street,
      Enticing the passer-by.
Not a child in the world but has flattened its nose
On its panes, gazing in, its small face in a muse,
Pining, wondering what to choose —
From Helen of Troy down to Margaret Rose. . . .

Nights in summer — how wan her stars!
      Her dark — how brief, and sweet!
Voices, past human wits to follow,
      Are heard where those waters meet.
The song of the bird in the silent hills
      Into the moonshine rills.

Old as they is that dark little house;
      But little a child can need
Is not to be bought there, for pennies, or love;
      And in gilded, outlandish screed,
Over its shutters — as if to rhyme! —
      Is the name of the Shop-keeper — TIME.

"ALL HOT"
(*The Chestnut Man*)

Brooding he stands,
And warms his hands
In this chill moonlit spot;
Cold to his feet
Is the cobbled street
And cold the north wind blows.
But his fire of coke —
Like rubies, look,
In Ali Baba's grot! —
Glows still and clear;
And children hear —
As dancing home from school they near —
His, " Chestnuts! Hot! All hot! "

That dog, called Jinks, who quietly blinks,
While toasting back and side,
Sits on in silence while he thinks,
And can at need *decide!*
He loves his slim Jemima,
But his collar can't abide.
So, one dark eye on her small thumb,
He waits his moment, sure to come,
When, tail and lead behind him,
With yelp of rapture off he goes,
Where nothing but his own sharp nose
Can ever hope to find him!

"PLEASE TO REMEMBER"

Here am I,
A poor old Guy:
Legs in a bonfire,
Head in the sky,

Shoeless my toes,
Wild stars behind,
Smoke in my nose,
And my eye-peeps blind;

Old hat, old straw —
In this disgrace;
While the wildfire gleams
On a mask for face.

Ay, all I am made of
Only trash is;
And soon — soon,
Will be dust and ashes.

THE LAMPLIGHTER

When the light of day declineth,
And a swift angel through the sky
Kindleth God's tapers clear,
With ashen staff the lamplighter
Passeth along the darkling streets
To light our earthly lamps;

Lest, prowling in the darkness,
The thief should haunt with quiet tread,
Or men on evil errands set;
Or wayfarers be benighted;
Or neighbours bent from house to house
Should need a guiding torch.

He is like a needlewoman
Who deftly on a sable hem
Stitches in gleaming jewels;
Or, haply, he is like a hero,
Whose bright deeds on the long journey
Are beacons on our way.

[35]

And when in the East cometh morning,
And the broad splendour of the sun,
Then, with the tune of little birds
Ringing on high, the lamplighter
Passeth by each quiet house,
And putteth out the lamps.

LOVELOCKS

I watched the Lady Caroline
Bind up her dark and beauteous hair;
Her face was rosy in the glass,
And 'twixt the coils her hands would pass,
    White in the candleshine.

Her bottles on the table lay,
Stoppered, yet sweet of violet;
Her image in the mirror stooped
To view those locks as lightly looped
    As cherry-boughs in May.

The snowy night lay dim without,
I heard the Waits their sweet song sing;
The windows smouldered keen with frost;
Yet still she twisted, sleeked and tossed
    Her beauteous hair about.

THE COMB

My mother sate me at her glass;
This necklet of bright flowers she wove;
Crisscrossed her gentle hands did pass,
And wound in my hair her love.

Deep in the mirror our glances met,
And grieved, lest from her care I roam,
She kissed me through her tears, and set
On high this spangling comb.

SEPHINA

Black lacqueys at the wide-flung door
Stand mute as men of wood.
Gleams like a pool the ball-room floor —
A burnished solitude.
A hundred waxen tapers shine
From silver sconces; softly pine
'Cello, fiddle, mandoline,
To music deftly wooed —
And dancers in cambric, satin, silk,
With glancing hair and cheeks like milk,
Wreathe, curtsey, intertwine.

[37]

The drowse of roses lulls the air
That's wafted up the marble stair.
Like warbling water clucks the talk.
From room to room in splendour walk
Guests, smiling in the silken sheen;
Carmine and azure, white and green,
They stoop and languish, pace and preen
Bare shoulder, painted fan,
Gemmed wrist and finger, neck of swan;
And still the plucked strings warble on;
Still from the snow-bowered, link-lit street
The muffled hooves of horses beat;
And harness rings; and foam-flecked bit
Clanks as the slim heads toss and stare
From deep, dark eyes. Smiling, at ease,
Mount to the porch the pomped grandees
In lonely state, by twos, and threes,
Exchanging languid courtesies,
While torches fume and flare.

And now the banquet calls. A blare
Of squalling trumpets clots the air;
And, flocking out, streams up the rout;
And lilies nod to velvet's swish.
And peacocks prim on gilded dish,
Vast pies thick-glazed, and gaping fish,
Towering confections crisp as ice,
Jellies aglare like cockatrice,
With thousand savours tongues entice.
Fruits of all hues, too, shape and bloom —
Pomegranate, quince and peach and plum,
Nectarine, grape, and cherry clear
And knotted pine — each leaf a spear . . .

And lo! — " La, la!
Mamma, mamma!
More marvellous lovely than a star
I see you standing there! . . ."

[38]

" Fie, fie Sephina! not in bed! "
Couched on the staircase overhead
Like ghost she gloats, her lean hand laid
On alabaster balustrade,
And gazes on and on;
Down on that wondrous to and fro
Till finger and foot are cold as snow
And half the night is gone;
And dazzled eyes are sore bestead,
Nods drowsily the sleek-locked head:
And, faint and far, spins, fading out
That rainbow-coloured, reeling rout
And, with faint sighs, her spirit flies
Into deep sleep. . . .
Come, Stranger, peep!
Was ever cheek so wan?

POOR "MISS 7"

Lone and alone she lies,
    Poor Miss 7,
Five steep flights from the earth,
    And one from heaven;
Dark hair and dark brown eyes, —
Not to be sad she tries,
Still — still it's lonely lies
    Poor Miss 7.

One day-long watch hath she,
    Poor Miss 7,
Not in some orchard sweet
    In April Devon, —
Just four blank walls to see,
And dark come shadowily,
No moon, no stars, ah me!
    Poor Miss 7.

[39]

And then to wake again,
    Poor Miss 7,
To the cold night — to have
    Sour physic given —
Out of some dream of pain;
Then strive long hours in vain
Deep dreamless sleep to gain:
    Poor Miss 7.

Yet memory softly sings
    Poor Miss 7
Songs full of love and peace
    And gladness even;
Clear flowers and tiny wings,
All tender, lovely things,
Hope to her bosom brings —
    Happy Miss 7.

Soldiers—Sailors—
Far Countries—
and the Sea

BLAISDELL

THE OLD SOLDIER

There came an Old Soldier to my door,
Asked a crust, and asked no more;
The wars had thinned him very bare,
Fighting and marching everywhere,
    With a Fol rol dol rol di do.

With nose stuck out, and cheek sunk in,
A bristling beard upon his chin —
Powder and bullets and wounds and drums
Had come to that Soldier as suchlike comes —
    With a Fol rol dol rol di do.

'Twas sweet and fresh with blossoming May,
Flowers springing from every spray;
And when he had supped the Old Soldier trolled
The song of youth that never grows old,
    Called Fol rol dol rol di do.

Most of him rags, and all of him lean,
And the belt round his belly drawn tightly in,
He lifted his peaked old grizzled head,
And these were the very same words he said —
    A Fol-rol-dol-rol-*di*-do.

THE PORTRAIT OF A WARRIOR

His brow is seamed with line and scar;
    His cheek is red and dark as wine;
The fires as of a Northern star
    Beneath his cap of sable shine.

His right hand, bared of leathern glove,
    Hangs open like an iron gin,
You stoop to see his pulses move,
    To hear the blood sweep out and in.

[43]

He looks some king, so solitary
    In earnest thought he seems to stand,
As if across a lonely sea
    He gazed impatient of the land.

Out of the noisy centuries
    The foolish and the fearful fade;
Yet burn unquenched these warrior eyes,
    Time hath not dimmed nor death dismayed.

THE SONG OF SOLDIERS

As I sat musing by the frozen dyke,
There was one man marching with a bright steel pike,
Marching in the dayshine like a ghost came he,
And behind me was the moaning and the murmur of the sea.

As I sat musing, 'twas not one but ten —
Rank on rank of ghostly soldiers marching o'er the fen,
Marching in the misty air they showed in dreams to me,
And behind me was the shouting and the shattering of the sea.

As I sat musing, 'twas a host in dark array,
With their horses and their cannon wheeling onward to the fray,
Moving like a shadow to the fate the brave must dree,
And behind me roared the drums, rang the trumpets of the sea.

MARCHING SONG

(From *The Three Royal Monkeys*)

Far away in Nanga-noon
Lived an old and grey Baboon,
Ah-mi, Sulâni!
Once a Prince among his kind,
Now forsaken, left behind,
Feeble, lonely, all but blind:
Sulâni, ghar magleer.

Peaceful Tishnar came by night,
In the moonbeams cold and white;
Ah-mi, Sulâni!
" Far away from Nanga-noon,
Old and lonely, grey Baboon;
Is a journey for thee soon!
Sulâni, ghar magleer.

" Be not frightened, shut thine eye;
Comfort take, nor weep, nor sigh;
Solitary Tishnar's nigh! "
Sulâni, ghar magleer.

Old Baboon, he gravely did
All that peaceful Tishnar bid;
Ah-mi, Sulâni!
In the darkness cold and grim
Drew his blanket over him;
Closed his old eyes, sad and dim:
Sulâni, ghar magleer.

Talaheeti sul magloon
Olgar, ulgar Nanga-noon;
Ah-mi, Sulâni!
Tishnar sootli maltmahee,
Ganganareez soongalee,
Manni Mulgar sang suwhee
Sulâni, ghar magleer.

CAPTAIN LEAN

Out of the East a hurricane
    Swept down on Captain Lean —
That mariner and gentleman
    Will not again be seen.

He sailed his ship against the foes
    Of his own country dear,
But now in the trough of the billows
    An aimless course doth steer.

Powder was violets to his nostrils,
    Sweet the din of the fighting-line,
Now he is flotsam on the seas,
    And his bones are bleached with brine.

The stars move up along the sky,
    The moon she shines so bright,
And in that solitude the foam
    Sparkles unearthly white.

This is the tomb of Captain Lean,
    Would a straiter please his soul?
I trow he sleeps in peace,
    Howsoever the billows roll!

GONE

Bright sun, hot sun, oh, to be
Where beats on the restless sea!
To hear the sirens of the deep
Chaunting old Ocean's floods
    to sleep!
And shadowed wave to sunlit
    wave
Call from the music-haunted cave!
There, with still eyes, their watch
    they keep,
While, at horizon mark, a ship,
With cloudlike sails glides slowly
    on,
    Smalls, vanishes, is gone.

THAMES

There flows a wonderful water
Where lofty vessels glide
To take up their home-come stations
By the dark wharves' side.
And their masts tip up over the roofs,
With their lean long pennons a-blow,
While ant-like the men on the stones of the quay
Swarm to and fro.
And their spars lean slant on the sky,
And strange are the sounds of their names,
Gilded on counters afloat from remote
Sea-havens to Thames.

SUNK LYONESSE

In sea-cold Lyonesse,
        When the Sabbath eve shafts down
On the roofs, walls, belfries
        Of the foundered town,
The Nereids pluck their lyres
        Where the green translucency beats,
And with motionless eyes at gaze
        Make minstrelsy in the streets.

The ocean water stirs
        In salt-worn casemate and porch
Plies the blunt-snouted fish
        With fire in his skull for torch.
And the ringing wires resound;
        And the unearthly lovely weep,
In lament of the music they make
        In the sullen courts of sleep.

Whose marble flowers bloom for aye,
        And — lapped by the moon-guiled tide —
Mock their carver with heart of stone,
        Caged in his stone-ribbed side.

MERMAIDS

Leagues, leagues over
The sea I sail
Couched on a walloping
Dolphin's tail:
The sky is on fire
The waves a-sheen;
I dabble my foot
In the billows green.

In a sea-weed hat
On the rocks I sit
Where tern and sea-mew
Glide and beat,
Where dark as shadows
The cormorants meet.

In caverns cool
When the tide's awash,
I sound my conch
To the watery splash.

From out their grottoes

At evening's beam
The mermaids swim
With locks agleam

To where I watch
On the yellow sands;
And they pluck sweet music
With sea-cold hands.

They bring me coral
And amber clear;
But when the stars
In heaven appear
Their music ceases,
They glide away,
And swim to their grottoes
Across the bay.

Then listen only
To my shrill tune
The surfy tide,
And the wandering moon.

THE SILVER PENNY

" Sailorman, I'll give to you
    My bright silver penny,
If out to sea you'll sail me
    And my dear sister Jenny."

" Get in, young sir, I'll sail ye
    And your dear sister Jenny,
But pay she shall her golden locks
    Instead of your penny."

They sail away, they sail away,
    O fierce the winds blew!
The foam flew in clouds
    And dark the night grew!

And all the green sea-water
    Climbed steep into the boat;
Back to the shore again
    Sail they will not.

Drowned is the sailorman,
    Drowned is sweet Jenny,
And drowned in the deep sea
    A bright silver penny.

WILD ARE THE WAVES

Wild are the waves when the wind blows;
But fishes in the deep
Live in a world of waters,
Still as sleep.

Wild are the skies when Winter
Roars at the doors of Spring;
But when his lamentation's lulled
Then sweet birds sing.

THE MERMAIDS

Sand, sand; hills of sand;
    And the wind where nothing is
Green and sweet of the land;
    No grass, no trees,
    No bird, no butterfly,
But hills, hills of sand,
    And a burning sky.

Sea, sea, mounds of the sea,
    Hollow, and dark, and blue,
Flashing incessantly
    The whole sea through;
    No flower, no jutting root,
Only the floor of the sea,
    With foam afloat.

Blow, blow, winding shells;
    And the watery fish,
Deaf to the hidden bells,
    In the water splash;
No streaming gold, no eyes,
    Watching along the waves,
But far-blown shells, faint bells,
    From the darkling caves.

ECHOES

The sea laments
The livelong day,
Fringing its waste of sand;
Cries back the wind from the whispering shore —
No words I understand:

Yet echoes in my heart a voice,
As far, as near, as these —
The wind that weeps,
The solemn surge
Of strange and lonely seas.

BONUM . OMEN

As we sailed out of London river,
Sing a lo lay and a lo lay lone,
I heard a Maid sing — " Come back, never! "
And a lo lay lone.

Her hair was yellow as sea-maids' hair is,
Sing a lo lay and a lo lay lone,
And she'd corn for the chicks that are Mother Carey's;
And a lo lay lone.

Sam Murphy's grog went cold as water,
Sing a lo lay and a lo lay lone,
And our hearts to our boots went tumbling after:
And a lo lay lone.

When we're there and back — by gum, we'll see her,
Sing a lo lay and a lo lay lone,
Buy cheap she may, but she sells de-ar:
And a lo lay lone.

THE O.M.O.R.E.

'Tis years fourscore
Since Rory O'More —
He and his brothers three,
Patrick, Seumas, and Timothy Tim,
With the Pole Star shining free,
Sailed with a sail, and an oar for a rudder,
Bound for an Unknown Sea.

Bound for that Unknown Sea forlore
Mariners many have sailed before;
Into the evening mist they swing,
Daring what ever the dark may bring;
And so went Timothy, Seumas and Pat,
Each with a sprig of yew in his hat,
And so sailed Rory O'More.

Sailed . . . But a wind came out of the cloud,
Piping shrill and long and loud,
Smote on their boat as they did float,
Stretched their cloaks on the stoop o' the wave,
Violet, azure, and green-grass-green,
And Rory's of scarlet brave;
Tossed them adrift on the foam of the main;
Bowed on them, fawned on them, bowed again,
Roared them to slumber, deep, serene,
Made of their sail their shroud . . .

Yet still 'tis whispered and still 'tis said
That fishermen weary and sore bestead,
Hauling their nets on the watery deep,
Numb with the cold and half asleep,
Will lift their eyes from the spray and spy
Ghosts in the glint of the moon pass by —
Phantoms four of the name of O'More,
Lifting their heads they see —
Patrick, Seumas, and Timothy Tim,
And Rory walking free,

Arm in arm where the petrels skim,
Over the billow's hissing rim,
Swinging their feet through the surge they go,
Four jolly ghosts in a glimmering row,
Four abreast, and nodding their heads,
Walking the waves these ghostly lads,
Haunting the wind with their voices four,
Timothy, Patrick, Seumas and Ror —
Rory O'More.

Striding the sea-drifts leagues from shore,
Ghosts of his brothers and Rory O'More
Fishermen white
In that haze of light
Dazed with its radiance, see,
And sigh in a breath,
Their beards beneath,
" See! there! — the O.M.O.R.E!
We have seen the O.M.O.R.E! "

ANDY BATTLE'S SONG

(From *The Three Royal Monkeys*)

Voice without a body,
Panther of black Roses,
Jack-Alls fat on icicles,
Ephelanto, Aligatha,
Zevvera and Jaccatray,
Unicorn and River-horse;
   Ho, ho, ho!
Here's Andy Battle,
Waiting for the enemy!

Imbe Calandola,
M'keesso and Quesanga,
Dondo, Sharamomba,
Pongo and Enjekko,
Millions of monkeys,
Rattlesnake and scorpion,
Swamp and death and shadow;
   Ho, ho, ho!
Come on, all of ye,
Here's Andy Battle,
Waiting and — alone!

WI'DECKS AWAS'

(Nod's song, from *The Three Royal Monkeys*)

Wi'decks awas'
Widevry sea,
An' flyin' scud
For companee,
Ole Ben, por Ben
Keepz watcherlone:
Boatz, zails, helmainmust,
Compaz gone.

Not twone ovall
'Is shippimuts can
Pipe pup ta prove
'Im livin' man:
One indescuppers

Flappziz 'and,
Fiss-like, as you
May yunnerstand.

An' one bracedup
Azzif to weat,
'Az aldy deck
For watery zeat;
Andwidda zteep
Unwonnerin' eye
Stares zon tossed sea
An' emputy zky.
Pore Benoleben,
Pore-Benn-ole-Ben!

YEO HO!

Once and there was a young sailor, yeo ho!
    And he sailed out over the say
For the isles where pink coral and palm branches blow,
    And the fire-flies turn night into day,
                Yeo ho!
And the fire-flies turn night into day.

But the *Dolphin* went down in a tempest, yeo ho!
    And with three forsook sailors ashore,
The *Portingales* took him where sugar-canes grow,
    Their slave for to be evermore,
                Yeo ho!
Their slave for to be evermore.

With his musket for mother and brother, yeo ho!
    He warred with the Cannibals drear,

In forests where panthers pad soft to and fro,
  And the *Pongo* shakes noonday with fear,
                    Yeo ho!

And the *Pongo* shakes noonday with fear.

Now lean with long travail, all wasted with woe,
  With a monkey for messmate and friend,
He sits 'neath the *Cross* in the cankering snow,
  And waits for his sorrowful end,
                    Yeo ho!

And waits for his sorrowful end.

THE PICTURE

  Here is a sea-legged sailor,
    Come to this tottering Inn,
Just when the bronze on its signboard is fading,
    And the black shades of evening begin.

  With his head on his paws sleeps a sheepdog,
    There stoops the Shepherd, and see,
All follow-my-leader the ducks waddle homeward,
    Under the sycamore tree.

  Burned brown is the face of the Sailor;
    His bundle is crimson; and green
Are the thick leafy boughs that hang dense o'er the Tavern;
    And blue the far meadows between.

But the Crust, Ale and Cheese of the Sailor,
    His Mug and his platter of Delf,
And the crescent to light home the Shepherd and Sheepdog
    The painter has kept to himself.

[55]

THE OLD SAILOR

There came an old sailor
Who sat to sup
Under the trees
Of the *Golden Cup*.

Beer in a mug
And a slice of cheese
With a hunk of bread
He munched at his ease.

Then in the summer
Dusk he lit
A little black pipe,
And sucked at it.

He thought of his victuals,
Of ships, the sea,
Of his home in the West,
And his children three.

And he stared and stared
To where, afar,
The lighthouse gleamed
At the harbour bar;

Till his pipe grew cold,
And down on the board
He laid his head,
And snored, snored, snored.

THE ENGLISHMAN

I met a sailor in the woods,
    A silver ring wore he,
His hair hung black, his eyes shone blue,
    And thus he said to me: —

" What country, say, of this round earth,
    What shore of what salt sea,
Be this, my son, I wander in,
    And looks so strange to me ? "

Says I, " O foreign sailorman,
    In England now you be,
This is her wood, and there her sky,
    And that her roaring sea."

He lifts his voice yet louder,
    " What smell be this," says he,
" My nose on the sharp morning air
    Snuffs up so greedily ? "

Says I, " It is wild roses
        Do smell so winsomely,
And winy brier too," says I,
        " That in these thickets be."

" And oh! " says he, " what leetle bird
        Is singing in yon high tree,
So every shrill and long-drawn note
        Like bubbles breaks in me? "

Says I, " It is the mavis
        That perches in the tree,
And sings so shrill, and sings so sweet,
        When dawn comes up the sea."

At which he fell a-musing,
        And fixed his eye on me,
As one alone 'twixt light and dark
        A spirit thinks to see.

" England! " he whispers soft and harsh,
        " England! " repeated he,
" And brier, and rose, and mavis,
        A-singing in yon high tree.

" Ye speak me true, my leetle son,
        So — so, it came to me,
A-drifting landwards on a spar,
        And grey dawn on the sea.

" Ay, ay, I could not be mistook;
        I knew them leafy trees,
I knew that land so witchery sweet,
        And that old noise of seas.

" Though here I've sailed a score of years,
        And heard 'em, dream or wake,
Lap small and hollow 'gainst my cheek,
        On sand and coral break;

[57]

" ' Yet now,' my leetle son, says I,
    A-drifting on the wave,
That land I see so safe and green
    Is England, I believe.

" ' And that there wood is English wood,
    And this here cruel sea,
The selfsame old blue ocean
    Years gone remembers me,

" ' A-sitting with my bread and butter
    Down behind yon chitterin' mill;
And this same Marinere ' — (that's me),
    ' Is that same leetle Will! —

" ' That very same wee leetle Will
    Eating his bread and butter there,
A-looking on the broad blue sea
    Betwixt his yaller hair! '

" And here be I, my son, throwed up
    Like corpses from the sea,
Ships, stars, winds, tempests, pirates past,
    Yet leetle Will I be! "

He said no more, that sailorman,
    But in a reverie
Stared like the figure of a ship
    With painted eyes to sea.

ARABY

" Dark-browed Sailor, tell me now,
Where, where is Araby?
The tide's aflow, the wind ablow,
'Tis I who pine for Araby."

" Master, she her spices showers
O'er nine and ninety leagues of sea;
The laden air breathes faint and rare —
Dreams on far-distant Araby."

" Oh, but Sailor, tell me true;
'Twas Man who mapped this Araby;
Though dangers brew, let me and you
Embark this night for Araby. . . ."

Wails the wind from star to star;
Rock the loud waves their dirge: and, see!
Through foam and wrack, a boat drifts back:
Ah, heart-beguiling Araby!

EDEN

I wonder if from Noah's Ark
Ever was heard the bobtail's bark.
If ever o'er the empty Flood
Our English ash-boughs stood in bud.
'Tis sure when Eve and Adam sate
Smiling within green Eden's gate
And gave its birds, beasts, fishes, names
Somewhere flowed clear our English Thames.
And when they both in woe were driven
Beyond the shining bounds of heaven,
Simply for grief that outcast morn
Broke into bloom our English thorn.
And — far from Eden — our nightingale
Did their sad banishment bewail:
While we, asleep within her dust,
Hearkened — as all poor humans must.

SAM

When Sam goes back in memory,
    It is to where the sea
Breaks on the shingle, emerald-green
    In white foam, endlessly;
He says — with small brown eye on mine —
    " I used to keep awake,
And lean from my window in the moon,
    Watching those billows break.
And half a million tiny hands,
    And eyes, like sparks of frost,
Would dance and come tumbling into the moon,
    On every breaker tossed.
And all across from star to star,
    I've seen the watery sea,
With not a single ship in sight,
    Just ocean there, and me;
And heard my father snore. . . And once,
    As sure as I'm alive,
Out of those wallowing, moon-flecked waves
    I saw a mermaid dive;
Head and shoulders above the wave,
    Plain as I now see you,
Combing her hair, now back, now front,
    Her two eyes peeping through;
Calling me, ' Sam! ' — quietlike — ' Sam! ' . . .
    But me . . . I never went,
Making believe I kind of thought
    'Twas someone else she meant . . .
Wonderful lovely there she sat,
    Singing the night away,
All in the solitudinous sea
    Of that there lonely bay.
P'raps," and he'd smooth his hairless mouth,
    " P'raps, if 'twere *now,* my son,
P'raps, if I heard a voice say, ' Sam! ' . . .
    Morning would find me gone."

THE WATER MIDDEN'S SONG

(From *The Three Royal Monkeys*)

Bubble, Bubble,
Swim to see
Oh, how beautiful
I be.

Fishes, Fishes,
Finned and fine,
What's your gold
Compared with mine?

Why, then, has
Wise Tishnar made
One so lovely
One so sad?

Lone am I,
And can but make
A little song,
For singing's sake.

BABEL

The sea washes England,
Where all men speak
A language rich
As ancient Greek.

The wide world over
Man with man
Has talked his own tongue
Since speech began.

Yet still must sorrow
Move the mind,

He understands
But his own kind.

The voices lovely,
Hollow, drear,
Of beast and bird
Beat on his ear:

Eye into eye
Gaze deep he may;
Yet still through Babel
Gropes his way.

King Canute
    Sat down by the sea,
Up washed the tide
    And away went he.

Good King Alfred
    Cried, " My sakes!
Not five winks,
    And look at those cakes! "

Lackland John
    Were a right royal Tartar
Till he made his mark
    Upon *Magna Carta:*

Ink, seal, table,
    On Runnymede green,
Anno Domini
    12–15.

THE LOST SHOE

Poor little Lucy
    By some mischance,
Lost her shoe
    As she did dance:

'Twas not on the stairs,
　Not in the hall;
Not where they sat
　At supper at all.
She looked in the garden,
　But there it was not;
Henhouse, or kennel,
　Or high dovecote.
Dairy and meadow,
　And wild woods through
Showed not a trace
　Of Lucy's shoe.
Bird nor bunny
　Nor glimmering moon
Breathed a whisper
　Of where 'twas gone.
It was cried and cried,
　Oyez and *Oyez!*
In French, Dutch, Latin
　And Portuguese.

Ships the dark seas
　Went plunging through,
But none brought news
　Of Lucy's shoe;
And still she patters,
　In silk and leather,
Snow, sand, shingle,
　In every weather;
Spain, and Africa,
　Hindustan,
Java, China,
　And lamped Japan,
Plain and desert,
　She hops — hops through,
Pernambuco
　To gold Peru;
Mountain and forest,
　And river too,
All the world over
　For her lost shoe.

THE ISLE OF LONE

Three dwarfs there were which lived in an isle,
　And the name of that isle was Lone,
And the names of the dwarfs were Alliolyle,
　Lallerie, Muziomone.

Their house was small and sweet of the sea,
　And pale as the Malmsey wine;
Their bowls were three, and their beds were three,
　And their nightcaps white were nine.

Their beds they were made of the holly-wood,
　Their combs of the tortoise-shell,
Three basins of silver in corners there stood,
　And three little ewers as well.

[63]

Green rushes, green rushes lay thick on the floor,
  For light beamed a gobbet of wax;
There were three wooden stools for whatever they wore
  On their humpity-dumpity backs.

So each would lie on a drowsy pillow
  And watch the moon in the sky —
And hear the parrot scream to the billow,
  And the billow roar reply.

Parrots of sapphire and sulphur and amber,
  Amethyst, azure and green,
While apes in the palm trees would scramble and clamber,
  Hairy and hungry and lean.

All night long with bubbles a-glisten
  The ocean cried under the moon,
Till ape and parrot too sleepy to listen
  To sleep and slumber were gone.

Then from three small beds the dark hours' while
  In a house in the Island of Lone
Rose the snoring of Lallerie, Alliolyle,
  The snoring of Muziomone.

But soon as ever came peep of sun
  On coral and feathery tree,
Three night-capped dwarfs to the surf would run
  And soon were a-bob in the sea.

At six they went fishing, at nine to snare
  Young foxes in the dells,
At noon in the shade on sweet fruits would fare,
  And blew in their twisted shells.

Dark was the sea they gambolled in,
  And thick with silver fish,
Dark as green glass blown clear and thin
  To be a monarch's dish.

They sate to sup in a jasmine bower,
  Lit pale with flies of fire,
Their bowls the hue of the iris-flower,
  And lemon their attire.

Sweet wine in little cups they sipped,
  And golden honeycomb
Into their bowls of cream they dipped,
  Whipt light and white as foam.

Now Alliolyle where the sand-flower blows
  Taught three old apes to sing —
Taught three old apes to dance on their toes
  And caper around in a ring.

They yelled them hoarse and they croaked them sweet,
  They twirled them about and around,
To the noise of their voices they danced with their feet,
  They stamped with their feet on the ground.

But down to the shore skipped Lallerie,
  His parrot on his thumb,
And the twain they scritched in mockery,
  While the dancers go and come.

And, alas! in the evening, rosy and still,
  Light-haired Lallerie
Bitterly quarrelled with Alliolyle
  By the yellow-sanded sea.

The rising moon swam sweet and large
  Before their furious eyes,
And they rolled and rolled to the coral marge
  Where the surf for ever cries.

Too late, too late, comes Muziomone:
  Clear in the clear green sea
Alliolyle lies not alone,
  But clasped with Lallerie.

He blows on his shell low plaintive notes;
  Ape, perequito, bee
Flock where a shoe on the salt wave floats, —
  The shoe of Lallerie.

He fetches nightcaps, one and nine,
  Grey apes he dowers three,
His house as fair as the Malmsey wine
  Seems sad as the cypress-tree.

Three bowls he brims with sweet honeycomb
  To feast the bumble-bees,
Saying, " O bees, be this your home,
  For grief is on the seas! "

He sate him down in a coral grot,
  At the flowing in of the tide;
When ebbed the billow, there was not,
  Save coral, aught beside.

So hairy apes in three white beds,
  And nightcaps, one and nine,
On moonlit pillows lay three heads
  Bemused with dwarfish wine.

A tomb of coral, the dirge of bee,
  The grey apes' guttural groan
For Alliolyle, for Lallerie,
  For thee, O Muziomone!

THE HORSEMAN

There was a Horseman rode so fast
The Sun in heaven stayed still at last.

On, on, and on, his galloping shoon
Gleamed never never beneath the Moon.

[66]

The People said, " Thou must be mad, O
Man with a never-lengthening shadow!

" Mad and bad! Ho! stay thy course,
Thou and thy never-stabled horse!

" Oh, what a wild and wicked sight —
A Horseman never dark with night!

" Depart from us, depart from us,
Thou and thy lank-maned Pegasus! " . . .

They talked into declining day,
Since both were now leagues — leagues away.

WHERE

Monkeys in a forest,
Beggermen in rags,
Marrow in a knucklebone,
Gold in leather bags;

Dumplings in the oven,
Fishes in a pool,
Flowers in a parlour,
Dunces in a school;

Feathers in a pillow,
Cattle in a shed,
Honey in a beehive,
    And Babs in bed.

All Creatures
Great and Small

SEEDS

The seeds I sowed —
For weeks unseen —
Have pushed up pygmy
Shoots of green;
So frail you'd think
The tiniest stone
Would never let
A glimpse be shown.

But no; a pebble
Near them lies,
At least a cherry-stone
In size,
Which that mere sprout
Has heaved away,
To bask in sunshine,
See the Day.

THE FLY

How large unto the tiny fly
    Must little things appear! —
A rosebud like a feather bed,
    Its prickle like a spear;

A dewdrop like a looking-glass,
  A hair like golden wire;
The smallest grain of mustard-seed
  As fierce as coals of fire;

A loaf of bread, a lofty hill;
  A wasp, a cruel leopard;
And specks of salt as bright to see
  As lambkins to a shepherd.

COME — GONE

Gone the snowdrop — comes the crocus;
With the tulip blows the squill;
Jonquil white as wax between them,
And the nid-nod daffodil.

Peach, plum, cherry, pear and apple,
Rain-sweet lilac on the spray;
Come the dog-rose in the hedges —
Gone's the sweetness of the may.

APPLE-FALL

Rosy the blossom that breaks in May;
  Autumn brings the apple;
Jackdaws in the belfry tower,
  Jackdaws in the steeple.
Comes a wind, blows a wind,
  Headlong down they tumble;
But bloom and berry share the sprig
  Of the prickly bramble.

A WIDOW'S WEEDS

A poor old Widow in her weeds
Sowed her garden with wild-flower seeds;
Not too shallow, and not too deep,
And down came April — drip — drip — drip.
Up shone May, like gold, and soon
Green as an arbour grew leafy June.
And now all summer she sits and sews
Where willow-herb, comfrey, bugloss blows
Teasel and tansy, meadowsweet,
Campion, toadflax, and rough hawksbit;
Brown bee orchis, and Peals of Bells;
Clover, burnet, and thyme she smells;
Like Oberon's meadows her garden is
Drowsy from dawn till dusk with bees.
Weeps she never, but sometimes sighs,
And peeps at her garden with bright brown eyes;
And all she has is all she needs —
A poor old Widow in her weeds.

THE HAREBELL

In the clear summer sunshine, hour by hour,
I've toiled, but toiled in vain, to paint this flower;
Brushes, and box of colours from their shelf,
And nought else with me but the flower itself.

Nothing alive — so steadfast yet so frail —
Could ever bloom on paper, I know well;
But poor and clumsy though the copy be,
I could not wish for happier company.

It seems it might, if I gazed on and on —
That wiry stalk, those petals, blue yet wan,
The solemn beauty of that marvellous cup —
At last, for very love, give its strange secret up.

[73]

THE ORCHARD

Lapped in the light and heat of noon,
I saw an orchard — glorious
With countless, cup-shaped, coloured flowers
Of intertwined convolvulus.

At sun-down, I came back again —
Faint shadows in the twilight wan;
A hundred aging apple trees;
But they? — all gone.

O DEAR ME!

Here are crocuses, white, gold, grey!
   " O dear me! " says Marjorie May;
Flat as a platter the blackberry blows:
   " O dear me! " says Madeleine Rose;
The leaves are fallen, the swallows flown:
   " O dear me! " says Humphrey John;
Snow lies thick where all night it fell:
   " O dear me! " says Emmanuel.

THE FLOWER

Listen, I who love thee well
Have travelled far, and secrets tell;
Cold the moon that gleams thine eyes,
Yet beneath her further skies
Rests, for thee, a paradise.

I have plucked a flower in proof,
Frail, in earthly light, forsooth:
See, invisible it lies
In this palm: now veil thine eyes:
Quaff its fragrancies!

[74]

Would indeed my throat had skill
To breathe thee music, faint and still —
Music learned in dreaming deep
In those lands, from Echo's lip. . . .
'Twould lull thy soul to sleep.

ECHO

" Who called ? " I said, and the words
        Through the whispering glades,
Hither, thither, baffled the birds —
        " Who called ? Who called ? "

The leafy boughs on high
        Hissed in the sun;
The dark air carried my cry
        Faintingly on:

Eyes in the green, in the shade,
        In the motionless brake,
Voices that said what I said,
        For mockery's sake:

" Who cares ? " I bawled through my tears;
        The wind fell low:
In the silence, " Who cares ? Who cares ? "
        Wailed to and fro.

TREES

Of all the trees in England,
        Her sweet three corners in,
Only the Ash, the bonnie Ash
        Burns fierce while it is green.

[75]

Of all the trees in England,
    From sea to sea again,
The Willow loveliest stoops her boughs
    Beneath the driving rain.

Of all the trees in England,
    Past frankincense and myrrh,
There's none for smell, of bloom and smoke,
    Like Lime and Juniper.

Of all the trees in England,
    Oak, Elder, Elm and Thorn,
The Yew alone burns lamps of peace
    For them that lie forlorn.

THE WIND

The wind — yes, I hear it — goes wandering by,
Willow and beech stir their branches and sigh;
Each leaf to its sister lisps softly, and then,
The air being stilled, they are silent again.

Alone with the stars stands a thorn on the height,
The snow of his flowers perfuming the night;
But so sharp are his prickles, so gnarled his old bole,
When the wind calls to him, he just whimpers, poor soul!

THE HOLLY

    The sturdiest of forest-trees
    With acorns is inset;
    Wan white blossoms the elder brings
    To fruit as black as jet;
    But O, in all green English woods
    Is aught so fair to view
    As the sleek, sharp, dark-leaved holly tree
    And its berries burning through?

Towers the ash; and dazzling green
The larch her tassels wears;
Wondrous sweet are the clots of may
The tangled hawthorn bears;
But O, in heath or meadow or wold
Springs aught beneath the blue
As brisk and trim as a holly-tree bole
With its berries burning through?

When hither, thither, falls the snow,
And blazes small the frost,
Naked amid the winter stars
The elm's vast boughs are tossed;
But O, of all that summer showed
What now to winter's true
As the prickle-beribbed dark holly tree,
With its berries burning through!

MRS. EARTH

Mrs. Earth makes silver black,
   Mrs. Earth makes iron red,
But Mrs. Earth cannot stain gold
   Nor ruby red.
Mrs. Earth the slenderest bone,
   Whitens in her bosom cold,
But Mrs. Earth can change my dreams
   No more than ruby or gold.
Mrs. Earth and Mr. Sun
   Can tan my skin, and tire my toes,
But all that I'm thinking of, ever shall think,
   Why, neither knows.

PRECIOUS STONES

Ruby, amethyst, emerald, diamond,
Sapphire, sardonyx, fiery-eyed carbuncle,
　　Jacynth, jasper, crystal a-sheen;
Topaz, turquoise, tourmaline, opal,
　　Beryl, onyx and aquamarine: —
Marvel, O mortal! — their hue, lustre, loveliness,
Pure as a flower when its petals unfurl —
Peach-red carnelian, apple-green chrysoprase,
　　Amber and coral and orient pearl!

NO JEWEL

No jewel from the rock
Is lovely as the dew,
Flashing with flamelike red
With sea-like blue.

No web the merchant weaves
Can rival hers —
The silk the spider spins
Across the furze.

THE POOL IN THE ROCK

In this water, clear as air,
Lurks a lobster in its lair.
Rock-bound weed sways out and in,
Coral-red, and bottle-green.
Wondrous pale anemones
Stir like flowers in a breeze:
Fluted scallop, whelk in shell,
And the prowling mackerel.
Winged with snow the sea-mews ride
The brine-keen wind; and far and wide
Sounds on the hollow thunder of the tide.

EARTH FOLK

The cat she walks on padded claws,
The wolf on the hills lays stealthy paws,
Feathered birds in the rain-sweet sky
At their ease in the air, flit low, flit high.

The oak's blind, tender roots pierce deep,
His green crest towers, dimmed in sleep,
Under the stars whose thrones are set
Where never prince hath journeyed yet.

ALL BUT BLIND

All but blind
    In his chambered hole
Gropes for worms
    The four-clawed Mole.

All but blind
    In the evening sky
The hooded Bat
    Twirls softly by.

All but blind
    In the burning day
The Barn-Owl blunders
    On her way.

And blind as are
    These three to me,
So, blind to Some-One
    I must be.

UNSTOOPING

Low on his fours the Lion
    Treads with the surly Bear;
But Men straight upward from the dust
    Walk with their heads in air;
The free sweet winds of heaven,
    The sunlight from on high
Beat on their clear bright cheeks and brows
    As they go striding by;
The doors of all their houses
    They arch so they may go,
Uplifted o'er the four-foot beasts,
    Unstooping, to and fro.

[79]

SHADOWS

The horse in the field,
The cows in the meadow,
Each browses and swishes
Plumb over its shadow —

It is noon. . . And beneath
That old thorn on the steep
A shepherd and sheepdog
Sit watching their sheep.

It is cool by the hedgerow,
A thorn for a tent,
Her flowers a snowdrift,
The air sweet with scent.

But oh, see already
The shade has begun
To incline to'rds the East,
As the earth and the sun

Change places, like dancers
In dance: for at morn
They stretched to the West —
When the new day was born.

NICHOLAS NYE

Thistle and darnel and dock grew there,
    And a bush, in the corner, of may,
On the orchard wall I used to sprawl
    In the blazing heat of the day;
Half asleep and half awake,
    While the birds went twittering by,
And nobody there my lone to share
    But Nicholas Nye.

Nicholas Nye was lean and grey,
    Lame of a leg and old,
More than a score of donkey's years
    He had seen since he was foaled;
He munched the thistles, purple and spiked,
    Would sometimes stoop and sigh,
And turn his head, as if he said,
      " Poor Nicholas Nye! "

Alone with his shadow he'd drowse in the meadow,
    Lazily swinging his tail,
At break of day he used to bray, —
    Not much too hearty and hale;
But a wonderful gumption was under his skin,
    And a clear calm light in his eye,
And once in a while: he'd smile . . .
      Would Nicholas Nye.

Seem to be smiling at me, he would,
    From his bush in the corner, of may, —
Bony and ownerless, widowed and worn,
    Knobble-kneed, lonely and grey;
And over the grass would seem to pass
    'Neath the deep dark blue of the sky,
Something much better than words between me
      And Nicholas Nye.

But dusk would come in the apple boughs,
    The green of the glow-worm shine,
The birds in nest would crouch to rest,
    And home I'd trudge to mine;
And there, in the moonlight, dark with dew,
    Asking not wherefore nor why,
Would brood like a ghost, and as still as a post.
      Old Nicholas Nye.

THE BANDOG

Has anybody seen my Mopser? —
    A comely dog is he,
With hair of the colour of a Charles the Fifth.
    And teeth like ships at sea,
His tail it curls straight upwards,
    His ears stand two abreast,
And he answers to the simple name of Mopser,
    When civilly addressed.

TOM'S LITTLE DOG

Tom told his dog called Tim to beg,
And up at once he sat,
His two clear amber eyes fixed fast,
His haunches on his mat.

Tom poised a lump of sugar on
His nose; then, " Trust! " says he;
Stiff as a guardsman sat his Tim;
Never a hair stirred he.

" Paid for! " says Tom; and in a trice
Up jerked that moist black nose;
A snap of teeth, a crunch, a munch,
And down the sugar goes!

FIVE EYES

In Hans' old mill his three black cats
Watch his bins for the thieving rats.
Whisker and claw, they crouch in the night,
Their five eyes smouldering green and bright:
Squeaks from the flour sacks, squeaks from where
The cold wind stirs on the empty stair,
Squeaking and scampering, everywhere.
Then down they pounce, now in, now out,
At whisking tail, and sniffing snout;
While lean old Hans he snores away
Till peep of light at break of day;
Then up he climbs to his creaking mill,
Out come his cats all grey with meal —
Jekkel, and Jessup, and one-eyed Jill.

PUSS

Puss loves man's winter fire
Now that the sun so soon
Leaves the hours cold it warmed
In burning June.

She purrs full length before
The heaped-up hissing blaze,

Drowsy in slumber down
Her head she lays.

While he with whom she dwells
Sits snug in his inglenook,
Stretches his legs to the flames
And reads his book.

SUPPER

Her pinched grey body,
In widow's fur,
Mousey daren't
From her wainscot stir;
Twitching nose,
And hollow ear,
She stoops and listens,
Stark with fear:

There, like a tiger,
Sleek and sly,
Grimalkin's crouched
With gloating eye,
Watching her door —
While over the crumbs
The dusk of deepening
Evening comes.

WHO REALLY?

When Winter's o'er, the Bear once more
Rolls from his hollow tree
And pokes about, and in and out.
Where dwells the honey-bee.
Then all the little creatures go,
And to their Queen they say:
" Here's that old Bruin, hark, what he's doing,
Let's drive the beast away! "
Old Bruin smiles, and smooths his hair
Over a sticky nose;
" That Thieves should hate a Thief," he smirks,
" Who really would suppose! "

[84]

OVER THE DOWNS
(For a Picture)

A stick between his knees, sits Pat,
And sugar-loaf in shape's his hat;
But Phil, his friend, has neither,
Unless to cool his fevered brow,
His hidden hat is off just now,
For warm in sooth's the weather.
Though Denton's seven miles away,
How sweet it is a while to be
At rest in this green solitude
Of peace and mystery! —
So still the very hares creep close,
As if in hope they can
By leaning their lank listening ears
His secrets share with Man.
What lies beyond that broken fence
When on we journey? Well,
The motionless bird upon the post
May know: he does not tell.

MASTER RABBIT

As I was walking,
Thyme sweet to my nose,
Green grasshoppers talking,
Rose rivalling rose:

Wings clear as amber,
Outspread in the light,
As from bush to bush
The Linnet took flight:

Master Rabbit I saw
In the shadow-rimmed mouth
Of his sandy cavern
Looking out to the South.

'Twas dew-tide coming,
The turf was sweet
To nostril, curved tooth,
And wool-soft feet.

Sun was in West,
Crystal in beam
Of its golden shower
Did his round eye gleam.

Lank horror was I,
And a foe, poor soul —
Snowy flit of a scut,
He was into his hole:

And — *stamp, stamp, stamp*
Through dim labyrinths clear —
The whole world darkened:
A Human near!

HI!

Hi! handsome hunting man
Fire your little gun.
Bang! Now the animal
Is dead and dumb and done.
Nevermore to peep again, creep again, leap again,
Eat or sleep or drink again, Oh, what fun!

DONE FOR

Old Ben Bailey
He's been and done
For a small brown bunny
With his long gun.

Glazed are the eyes
That stared so clear,
And no sound stirs
In that hairy ear.

What was once beautiful
Now breathes not,
Bound for Ben Bailey's
Smoking pot.

[86]

TIT FOR TAT

Have you been catching of fish, Tom Noddy?
    Have you snared a weeping hare?
Have you whistled, " No Nunny," and gunned a poor bunny,
    Or a blinded bird of the air?

Have you trod like a murderer through the green woods,
    Through the dewy deep dingles and glooms,
While every small creature screamed shrill to Dame Nature,
    " He comes — and he comes! "?

Wonder I very much do, Tom Noddy,
    If ever, when off you roam,
An Ogre from space will stoop a lean face
    And lug you home:

Lug you home over his fence, Tom Noddy,
    Of thorn-sticks nine yards high,
With your bent knees strung round his old iron gun
    And your head dan-dangling by:

And hang you up stiff on a hook, Tom Noddy,
    From a stone-cold pantry shelf,
Whence your eyes will glare in an empty stare,
    Till you are cooked yourself!

FOXES

Old Dr. Cox's
Love of foxes
Led his steps astray;
He'd haunt the woods and coppices,
And lure the beasts away,
Into a bright green private park,
In safety there to *stay*.

Now Dr. Cox's
Dodge with foxes
Was simple as could be;
For first of all he'd find an earth,
And mark it with a T
(Just T for Trapper); then he'd wait
Till dusk; just wait and see.

For Dr. Cox's
Way with foxes
Needed but a *hush;*
When seated on a bank of loam,
Beneath a tree or bush,
He'd tootle-ootle on a comb,
And each would bring its brush.

THE GREY WOLF

" A faggot, a faggot, go fetch for the fire, son! "
" O, Mother, the wolf looks in at the door! "
" Cry Shoo! now, cry Shoo! thou fierce grey wolf, fly, now;
Haste thee away, he will fright thee no more."

" I ran, O, I ran but the grey wolf ran faster,
O, Mother, I cry in the air at thy door,
Cry Shoo! now, cry Shoo! but his fangs were so cruel,
Thy son (save his hatchet) thou'lt never see more."

THE GAGE

" Lady Jane, O Lady Jane!
Your hound hath broken bounds again,
   And chased my timorous deer, O;
     If him I see,
     That hour he'll dee;
My brakes shall be his bier, O."

" Hoots! lord, speak not so proud to me!
My hound, I trow, is fleet and free,
   He's welcome to your deer, O;
     Shoot, shoot you may,
     He'll gang his way,
Your threats we nothing fear, O."

He's fetched him in, he's laid him low,
Drips his lifeblood red and slow,
   Darkens his dreary eye, O;
     " Here is your beast,
     And now at least
My herds in peace shall lie, O."

" ' In peace! ' my lord, O mark me well!
For what my jolly hound befell
   You shall sup twenty-fold, O!
     For every tooth
     Of his, i'sooth,
A stag in pawn I hold, O.

" Huntsman and horn, huntsman and horn,
Shall scour your heaths and coverts lorn,
   Baying them shrill and clear, O:
     But lone and still
     Shall lift each hill,
Each valley wan and sere, O.

" Ride up you may, ride down you may,
Lonely or trooped, by night or day,
　　One ghost shall haunt you ever:
　　　　Bird, beast, and game
　　　　Shall dread the same,
The fish of lake and river."

Her cheek burns angry as the rose,
Her eye with wrath and pity flows:
　　She gazes fierce and round, O.
　　　　" Dear Lord! " he says,
　　　　" What loveliness
To waste upon a hound, O!

" I'd give my stags, my hills and dales,
My stormcocks and my nightingales
　　To have undone this deed, O;
　　　　For deep beneath
　　　　My heart is death
Which for her love doth bleed, O."

He wanders up, he wanders down,
On foot, on horse, by night and noon;
　　His lands are bleak and drear, O;
　　　　Forsook his dales
　　　　Of nightingales,
Forsook his moors of deer, O.

Forsook his heart, ah me! of mirth;
There's nothing precious left on earth;
　　All happy dreams seem vain, O,
　　　　Save where remote
　　　　The moonbeams gloat,
And sleeps the lovely Jane, O.

But happed one eve alone he went,
Gnawing his beard in dreariment —

Lo! from a thicket hidden,
　　Lovely as flower
　　In April hour,
Steps forth a form unbidden.

" Get ye now down, my lord, to me!
I'm troubled so I'm like to dee,"
　　She cries, 'twixt joy and grief, O;
　　　" The hound is dead,
　　　When all is said,
But love is past belief, O.

" Nights, nights I've lain your lands to see,
Forlorn and still — and all for me,
　　All for a foolish curse, O;
　　　Pride may be well,
　　　But truth to tell,
To live unloved is worse, O! "

In faith, this lord, in that lone dale,
Hears now a sweeter nightingale,
　　And lairs a tenderer deer, O;
　　　His sorrow goes
　　　Like mountain snows
In waters sweet and clear, O!

And now, what hound is this that fleet
Comes fawning to his mistress' feet,
　　And's bid forgive a master?
　　　How swiftly love
　　　May grief remove,
How happy make disaster!

Ay, as it were a bud did break
To loveliness for pity's sake,
　　So she in beauty moving
　　　Rides at his hand
　　　Across his land,
Beloved as well as loving.

THE PIGS AND THE CHARCOAL-BURNER

The old Pig said to the little pigs,
    " In the forest is truffles and mast,
Follow me then, all ye little pigs,
    Follow me fast! "

The Charcoal-burner sat in the shade,
    His chin on his thumb,
And saw the big Pig and the little pigs,
    Chuffling come.

He watched 'neath a green and giant bough,
    And the pigs in the ground
Make a wonderful grisling and gruzzling
    And greedy sound.

And when, full-fed, they were gone, and Night
    Walked her starry ways,
He stared with his cheeks in his hands
    At his sullen blaze.

MARCH HARES

" The best way to go," said my muffled-up friend, " is to look in its
    form for a Hare, you know ";
So, with gun over shoulder, we sallied out early, the bushes all
    hunched up with snow, you know;
The dawn was still under the eastern horizon, and O but the morn-
    ing was rare, you know;
The elms and the oaks were a-dangle with ice, that swayed in the
    breeze to and fro, you know —
Icicles half a yard long at the least, that tinkled and rang in the air,
    you know;
" A marvellous music," said I to my friend; and he, he never said,
    No, you know.

The snow had been falling for days — there were drifts full fifteen feet deep, and so fair, you know,
Aurora herself might have looked to her blushes, and Cupid have trimmed up his bow, you know;
And when o'er the rim of the World came the Sun and with eye like a topaz did glare, you know,
We stood for a while as if blinded with Paradise, dumb in that wonderful glow, you know;
We coughed, and we shifted our guns, and went on — no more than a cough could we dare, you know.
For moment by moment we couldn't tell where we should come within sight of the foe, you know.

And, all of a sudden, my friend, he said, " Ssh! " and I looked and I listened; and there, you know —
Not half a shot off, with his ears and his scut, crouching close in the lily-white snow, you know,
And his eyes like two blazing bright marbles of glass — sat staring and glaring a Hare, you know!
The sun it shone brighter, the blue it grew bluer, the heavens like an infinite O, you know,
And a breeze out of nowhere rang sweet as a bell rings, and stirred in our whiskers and hair, you know.

My friend — then — he — up — with — his — gun — to — his — shoulder — and tugged at the trigger: but lo! you know
In his kindness of heart he'd forgotten to load, for for slaughter he didn't much care, you know;
We laughed, oh! laughed we; and, my ghost! if old Watt didn't up with his nose and cry, " Ho! " you know;
And stamped for his brothers and sisters to come; and they hopped up in scores from their lairs, you know.
They danced, they fandangoed, they scuttered, they sang, turned somersaults, leapfrogged, and so, you know
We trudged back to breakfast with nothing to jug, which wasn't *exactly* fair, you know,
　　Which *wasn't* exactly fair.

THE SHIP OF RIO

There was a ship of Rio
    Sailed out into the blue,
And nine and ninety monkeys
    Were all her jovial crew.
From bo'sun to the cabin boy,
    From quarter to caboose,
There weren't a stitch of calico
    To breech 'em — tight or loose;
From spar to deck, from deck to keel,
    From barnacle to shroud,
There weren't one pair of reach-me-downs
    To all that jabbering crowd.
But wasn't it a gladsome sight,
    When roared the deep-sea gales
To see them reef her fore and aft,
    A-swinging by their tails!
Oh, wasn't it a gladsome sight,
    When glassy calm did come,
To see them squatting tailor-wise
    Around a keg of rum!
Oh, wasn't it a gladsome sight,
    When in she sailed to land,
To see them all a-scampering skip
    For nuts across the sand!

THE PRINCE

Sweet Peridarchus was a Prince,
The Prince he was of — Mouses;
He roved and roamed the haunts of Men,
And ranged about their houses.

He gnawed his way along a street,
Through holes in every wainscot,
Fandangoed in the attics and
From basement on to basement.

His eyes like bits of rubies shone;
His coat, as sleek as satin,
With teeth as sharp as needle-points
He kept to keep him fat in.

His squeak so sharp in the small hours rang
That every waker wondered;
He trimmed his whiskers stiff as wire,
Had sweethearts by the hundred.

He'd gut a Cheshire cheese with ease,
Plum cake devoured in slices,
Lard, haggis, suet, sausages,
And everything that nice is.

Cork out, he'd dangle down his tail
For oil that was in bottle;
Nothing too sweet, nothing too fat
For Peridarchus' throttle.

He'd dance upon a chimney-pot,
The merry stars a-twinkling;
Or, scampering up a chandelier,
Set all the lustres tinkling.

He'd skip into a pianoforté
To listen how it sounded;
He bored into a butt of wine,
And so was nearly drownded.

At midnight when he sat at meat,
Twelve saucy sonsy maidens,
With bee-sweet voices ditties sang,
Some sad ones, and some gay ones.

For bodyguard he had a score
Of warriors grim and hardy;
They raided every larder round,
From Peebles to Cromàrty.

Grimalkin — deep in dreams she lay,
Comes he, with these gay friskers,
Steals up and gnaws away her claws,
And plucks out all her whiskers.

He scaled a bell-rope where there snored
The Bailiff and his Lady;
Danced on his nose, nibbled her toes,
And kissed the squalling Baby.

A merry life was his, I trow,
Despite it was a short one;
One night he met a mort of rats —
He bared his teeth, and fought one:

A bully ruffian, thrice his size;
But when the conflict ended,
He sighed, " Alack, my back is broke,
And that can ne'er be mended."

They laid him lifeless on a bier,
They lapped him up in ermine;
They lit a candle, inches thick,
His Uncle preached the sermon: —

" O Mouseland, mourn for him that's gone,
Our noble Peridarchus!
In valiant fight but yesternight,
And now, alas, a carcass!

" A Hero — Mouse or Man — is one
Who never wails or winces;
Friends, shed a tear for him that's here,
The Princeliest of Princes! "

THE ACCOMPANIMENT
(*For a Woodcut*)

The man in the hat (whom you see in the picture)
    Mused softly one evening: " I sit in this copse,
And the birds warble sweetly, for sweet is their nature;
    Yet they sing at haphazard: then — every one stops.

" Yes, as if at the lift of a baton or finger,
    The love-notes, *pu-wees,* and *too-witta-woos* cease,
Not a pause for applause, not a wing seems to linger,
    The forests fall mute — the whole world is at peace.

" I marvel. I marvel. For take, now, the linnet —
    That sociable haunter of charlock and gorse,
There is no sweeter throat with a melody in it,
    Still, *solo* he pipes as a matter of course!

" God forbid that with drum, cornet, triangle, cymbal,
    We should drown the wee cherubs. Assuredly not.
Still, my dear sister Jane on the harp is still nimble,
    Nor have I my old skill with the fiddle forgot . . ."

So now, as the sun in the West is declining,
    The twain to that hill hie, the birds hie there too;
Rings the plucking of harp-strings, the catgut's sweet pining,
    And a chorus *orchestral* ascends to the blue.

Besides which, a host of all small kinds of beasties,
    (They are shown on the cut, though Miss Jane's out of sight),
Having learned the harmonic a marvellous feast is,
    Troll out an *Amen* ere they part for the night.

DUCKS

(For a Picture)

See, now, a child must this way come —
    And early out of bed! —
Who, still with dreams in his bright eyes,
    Has filled a bag with bread,
And scampers down to feed the Ducks,
    All flocking to be fed.
The tiny man in that tiny boat,
Upon that placid lake afloat,
Is looking back, and so can see
Many now hidden from you and me;
And these, like ours, no doubt he finds
Of several sizes, shapes and *kinds:* —

The Farmyard Duck is white as snow;
    And quacks a merry quack;
    The Tufted wears a topknot;
    The Labrador is black;
The Pochard, and the Goldeneye
    As soon as seen are gone:
Like fish-with-wings they cruise beneath
    The water else they are *on*.

The wild, wild Mallard in chestnut flies,
    Steel-blue, and emerald green;
Low head outstretched, and bead-dark eyes,
He arrows through the empty skies,
    As evening dusk sets in.
The Pintail whistles to the wind;
The Shoveller calls " puck-puck ";
The downy Eider an island loves
    And shares a sailor's luck;
The wary Widgeon will talk all day,
    Then sleep on a stormy sea;
But the Teal nests inland, and at peace —
    A loving mother she.

And one a bill has like a hook;
    And one like a flattened spoon:
They gossip, paddle, dive and bask —
    Pond, ocean, stream, lagoon:
On snails or plants or fishes feed,
Worms, insects, frogs, or water-weed,
As does, according to his need,
    The lovelorn Mandarin.

All these are *kinds*. But every Duck
Himself is, and himself alone:
Fleet wing, arched neck, webbed foot, round eye,
    And marvellous cage of bone.
Clad in this beauty a creature dwells,
Of sovran instinct, sense and skill;
Yet secret as the hidden wells
    Whence Life itself doth rill.

QUACK-HUNTING

When evening's darkening azure
    Stains the water crystal clear,
It's a marvellous sweet pleasure
    A small coracle to steer
To where, in reeds and rushes,
    Squeak and chuckle, sup and suck
A multitudinous company
    Of Duck.

There silver-shining Hesper
    Smiles at Mars — a solemn red;
The myriads of the Milky Way
    Are circling overhead;
But even though the dusk's too dim
    To sheen their wings — with luck
I catch those button eyes and know
    They're Duck.

[99]

Not mine the dismal fowling-piece,
  The *living* duck for me!
I strow upon the water crumbs
  Which they, that instant, see;
They paddle in like steamboats, with
  Their tails behind their backs;
And I? I simply sit and count
  Their quacks.

One sigh in that great silence —
  Wild-winged creatures, they'd be gone!
But me — I scarcely breathe, I don't,
  But softly sidle on;
And while the dears are feeding, with
  Their tails behind their backs,
I make my nightly score, I count
  Their quacks.

CHICKEN

Clapping her platter stood plump Bess,
 And all across the green
Came scampering in, on wing and claw,
 Chicken fat and lean: —
Dorking, Spaniard, Cochin China,
 Bantams sleek and small,
Like feathers blown in a great wind,
 They came at Bessie's call.

GRACE

For every sip the Hen says grace;
The Rabbit twinkles his small face;
Ev'n to the Fox, stol'n safely home,
A crafty grin of thanks must come;
Even the Spider, plump in net,
His manners cannot quite forget,
And when he's supped upon a fly
Puts what is over neatly by.
Oh, *any* one with tongue and wits
Who crowded up with victuals sits
Through breakfasts, luncheons, dinners, teas,
With never a *Thank you* or a *Please,*
Eating not what he should but can,
Can *not* be a well-mannered man.
No doubt if Cows and Sheep were able
To draw their chairs up to the table,
It's only common sense to say
They'd keep on stuffing there all day,
They need such quantities of hay.
But though they never could let pass
A dainty dish of greens or grass,
Even the littlest Lambkin would
Express a sheepish gratitude;
While sager beasts, however staid,
Might smile upon the parlourmaid.

THE MOTHER BIRD

Through the green twilight of a hedge
I peered, with cheek on the cool leaves pressed,
And spied a bird upon a nest:
Two eyes she had beseeching me
Meekly and brave, and her brown breast
Throbb'd hot and quick above her heart;

And then she opened her dagger bill, —
'Twas not the chirp that sparrows pipe
At early day; 'twas not the trill,
That falters through the quiet even;
But one sharp solitary note,
One desperate fierce and vivid cry
Of valiant tears, and hopeless joy,
One passionate note of victory.
Off, like a fool afraid, I sneaked,
Smiling the smile the fool smiles best,
At the mother bird in the secret hedge
Patient upon her lonely nest.

THE THRUSH

Even earlier yet this listening thrush —
    Alone on her leafy bough —
Trilled out her brier-sweet song of praise
To greet the risen sun; and now,
With glittering eye and speckled breast,
Peeps this way, that way, then at nest,
As though, for joy, she is not sure
If it hold one egg less — or more,
    Since last she counted four.

How strange that one, of shade the lover,
Has chosen a tree so spare in cover!
But had she built to shield her brood
In laurel bush, or ivy-tod,
Her plaited nest so plainly seen
Would hidden out of sight have been.
Nor could a watch be kept so well
When her first young one cracks its shell;
Nor on all four when, fledged, they fly,
And — later eggs being hatched — will try
To help her feed her family!

JENNIE WREN

That farthing bird, J. Wren,
The cruel boys pursue;
Hunt her with sticks and stones
Hedge and green coppice through.

A farthing bird. Amen.
Ay, two brown sparrows can
For as easy a sum be bought
By heedless chaffering man.

Yet not for all earthbound gold,
Or argosies under the sea,
Can one moment's pity of pitiful child
Be marketed for, perdie.

THE ROBIN

As little Bess was walking home
She saw a robin on a stone.
He looked at her with bead-bright eye —
These two alone there, no one by.

She gave him bread-crumbs dipped in milk,
She stroked his feathers soft as silk.
Then leaning sidelong her fair head,
" Sing, sweet! I'm listening," she said.

And he, the dainty imp, he skips,
And pecks a crumb between her lips
And then, to his own wild being gone,
Left empty the round pebble-stone.

A GOLDFINCH

This feather-soft creature
Tail to head,
Is golden yellow,
And black, and red.

A sip of water,
A twig to sing on,

A prong for nest,
The air to wing on,

A mate to love,
Some thistledown seed
Are all his joy, life,
Beauty, need.

THE BIRD SET FREE

" No marvel, Sweet, you clap your wings
In hunger for the open sky;
I see your pretty flutterings,
Will let you fly.

" But O, when in some shady grot
You preen your breast in noonday's blue,
Be not your Susan quite forgot,
Who hungers too! "

A WARBLER

In the sedge a tiny song
Wells and trills the whole day long;
In my heart another bird
Has its music heard.

As I watch and listen here,
Each to each pipes low and clear;
But when one has ceased to sing,
Mine will still be echoing.

TINY EENANENNIKA

Tiny Eenanennika
Was like a little bird;
If the least whisper sounded,
She heard, oh, she heard!
Claw or wing, in bush or brake,
However soft it stirred.

Tiny Eenanennika
Had bright gold hair;
Fair as a field of wheat,
Like sunshine, fair,
Like flame, like gilded water — oh,
Past words to declare!

And every sing-song bird there is,
Titmouse to wren,
In springtime, in nesting-time,
Would watch keep; and when
She chanced to look the other way
Would steal up, and then —

Snip from her shining head
Just one hair, or twain,
A gleaming, glistening, shimmering thread,
And fly off again —
A gossamer of glittering gold,
And flit off again.

THE FEATHER

A feather, a feather! —
I wonder whether
Of Wren? Or Sparrow?
Or poor Cock Robin,
Shot with an arrow?

A learnèd man
Would tell me whether
This airy scrap
Of down — this feather,
Was of Wren, or Sparrow —
From thorn or willow,
Ivy or gorse,
Or grey-leafed sallow —
Or poor Cock Robin's,
Shot with an arrow.

The beak nibs in,
A wind-puff blows,
Off and away
The morsel goes,
Tiny, delicate,
Downy, narrow,
Preened and sleek —
The dainty fellow!

So I can't help asking,
Wren? Or Sparrow?
Or — it would fill
My heart with sorrow —
Poor Cock Robin's,
Slain with an arrow?

MISSEL THRUSH

When from the brittle ice the fields
Begin to spring with green,
Then sits the storm-cock tree-top high,
And shrills the blasts between.

And when the sun, with thinning ray,
Tells winter's drawing nigh,
Still, this wild bird, of valiant heart,
Shouts wild against the sky.

THE STORM

First there were two of us, then there were three of us,
Then there was one bird more,
Four of us — wild white sea-birds,
Treading the ocean floor;
And the *wind* rose, and the *sea* rose,
To the angry billows' roar —
With one of us — two of us — three of us — four of us
Sea-birds on the shore.

Soon there were five of us, soon there were nine of us,
And lo! in a trice sixteen!
And the yeasty surf curdled over the sands,
The gaunt grey rocks between;
And the tempest raved, and the lightning's fire
Struck blue on the spindrift hoar —
And on four of us — ay, and on four times four of us
Sea-birds on the shore.

And our sixteen waxed to thirty-two,
And they to past three score —
A wild, white welter of winnowing wings,
And ever more and more;
And the winds lulled, and the sea went down,
And the sun streamed out on high,
Gilding the pools and the spume and the spars
'Neath the vast blue deeps of the sky;

And the isles and the bright green headlands shone,
As they'd never shone before,
Mountains and valleys of silver cloud,
Wherein to swing, sweep, soar —
A host of screeching, scolding, scrabbling
Sea-birds on the shore —
A snowy, silent, sun-washed drift
Of sea-birds on the shore.

THE BORDER BIRD

As if a voice had called, I woke,
The world in silence lay;
The winter sun was not yet up,
The moon still in the sky.

A strange sea-bird had hither flown,
Out of the last of night,
While yet the Dog Star in the West
Shone palely bright.

His wings came like a *hush* of wind,
His feet were coral red,
No mantling swan has softer down,
No blackcap blacker head.

He lighted on the frozen snow;
Trod here, and there, and then
Lifted his gentle neck and gazed
Up at my window-pane.

And I, from out of dream, looked down,
This lovely thing to see;
The world a wilderness of white,
Nought living there but he.

Then with a sweet low call, he raised
Dark head and pinions wan,
Swept up into the gold of day,
   Was gone.

Fairies—
Witches—Phantoms

SLEEPYHEAD

As I lay awake in the white moonlight,
I heard a faint singing in the wood,
   " Out of bed,
   Sleepyhead,
   Put your white foot now,
   Here are we,
   Neath the tree
   Singing round the root now! "

I looked out of window, in the white moonlight,
The trees were like snow in the wood —
   " Come away,
   Child, and play
   Light with the gnomies;
   In a mound,
   Green and round,
   That's where their home is.

   " Honey sweet,
   Curds to eat,
   Cream and fruménty,
   Shells and beads,
   Poppy seeds,
   You shall have plenty."

But soon as I stooped in the dim moonlight
To put on my stocking and my shoe,
The sweet sweet singing died sadly away,
And the light of the morning peeped through:
Then instead of the gnomies there came a red robin
To sing of the buttercups and dew.

A–TISHOO

" Sneeze, Pretty: sneeze, Dainty,
Else the Elves will have you sure,
Sneeze, Light-of-Seven-Bright-Candles,
See they're tippeting at the door;
Tiny feet in measure falling,
All their little voices calling,
Calling, calling, calling, calling —
Sneeze, or never come no more! "
    " *A-tishoo!* "

BLUEBELLS

Where the bluebells and the wind are,
Fairies in a ring I spied,
And I heard a little linnet
Singing near beside.

Where the primrose and the dew are,
Soon were sped the fairies all:
Only now th green turf freshens,
And the linnets call.

THE BUCKLE

I had a silver buckle,
I sewed it on my shoe,
And 'neath a sprig of mistletoe
I danced the evening through!

I had a bunch of cowslips,
I hid 'em in a grot,
In case the elves should come by night
And me remember not.

I had a yellow riband,
I tied it in my hair,
That, walking in the garden,
The birds might see it there.

I had a secret laughter,
I laughed it near the wall:
Only the ivy and the wind
May tell of it at all.

THE HORN

Hark! is that a horn I hear,
    In cloudland winding sweet —
And bell-like clash of bridle-rein,
    And silver-shod light feet

Is it the elfin laughter
    Of fairies riding faint and high,
Beneath the branches of the moon,
    Straying through the starry sky?

Is it in the globèd dew
    Such sweet melodies may fall?
Wood and valley — all are still,
    Hushed the shepherd's call.

THE FAIRIES DANCING

I heard along the early hills,
Ere yet the lark was risen up,
Ere yet the dawn with firelight fills
The night-dew of the bramble-cup, —
I heard the fairies in a ring
Sing as they tripped a lilting round
Soft as the moon on wavering wing.
The starlight shook as if with sound,
As if with echoing, and the stars
Pranked their bright eyes with trembling gleams;
While red with war the gusty Mars
Rained upon earth his ruddy beams.
He shone alone, low down the West,
While I, behind a hawthorn-bush,
Watched on the fairies flaxen-tressed
The fires of the morning flush.
Till, as a mist, their beauty died,
Their singing shrill and fainter grew;
And daylight tremulous and wide
Flooded the moorland through and through;
Till Urdon's copper weathercock
Was reared in golden flame afar,
And dim from moonlit dreams awoke
The towers and groves of Arroar.

DOWN–ADOWN–DERRY

Down-adown-derry,
Sweet Annie Maroon,
Gathering daisies
In the meadows of Doone,
Sees a white fairy
Skip buxom and free
Where the waters go brawling
In rills to the sea;
    Singing down-adown-derry.

Down-adown-derry,
Sweet Annie Maroon
Through the green grasses
Peeps softly; and soon
Spies under green willows
A fairy whose song
Like the smallest of bubbles
Floats bobbing along;
    Singing down-adown-derry.

Down-adown-derry
Her cheeks are like wine,
Her eyes in her wee face
Like water-sparks shine,
Her niminy fingers
Her sleek tresses preen,
The which in the combing
She peeps out between;
    Singing down-adown-derry.

" Down-adown-derry,"
And shrill was her tune: —
" Come to my water-house,
Annie Maroon,
Come in your dimity,
Ribbon on head,
To wear siller seaweed
And coral instead;
    Singing down-adown-derry."

" Down-adown-derry,
Lean fish of the sea,
Bring lanthorns for feasting
The gay Faërie;
'Tis sand for the dancing,
A music all sweet
In the water-green gloaming
For thistledown feet;
    Singing down-adown-derry."

Down-adown-derry,
Sweet Annie Maroon
Looked large on the fairy
Curled wan as the moon;
And all the grey ripples
To the Mill racing by,
With harps and with timbrels
Did ringing reply;
    Singing down-adown-derry.

" Down-adown-derry,"
Sang the Fairy of Doone,
Piercing the heart
Of Sweet Annie Maroon;
And lo! when like roses
The clouds of the sun
Faded at dusk, gone
Was Annie Maroon;
    Singing down-adown-derry.

Down-adown-derry,
The daisies are few;
Frost twinkles powd'ry
In haunts of the dew;
And only the robin
Perched on a thorn,
Can comfort the heart
Of a father forlorn;
    Singing down-adown-derry.

Down-adown-derry
Snow's on the air;
Ice where the lily
Bloomed waxen and fair;
He may call o'er the water,
Cry — cry through the Mill.
But Annie Maroon, alas!
Answer ne'er will;
    Singing down-adown-derry.

THE BEES' SONG

Thousandz of thornz there be
On the Rozez where gozez
The Zebra of Zee:
Sleek, striped, and hairy,
The steed of the Fairy
Princess of Zee.

Heavy with blossomz be
The Rozez that growzez
In the thickets of Zee.
Where grazez the Zebra,
Marked *Abracadeeebra*
Of the Princess of Zee.

And he nozez the poziez
Of the Rozez that growzez
So luvez'm and free,
With an eye, dark and wary,
In search of a Fairy,
Whose Rozez he knowzez
Were not honeyed for he,
But to breathe a sweet incense
To solace the Princess
Of far-away Zzzee.

THE HONEY ROBBERS

There were two Fairies, Gimmul and Mel,
Loved Earth Man's honey passing well;
Oft at the hives of his tame bees
They would their sugary thirst appease.

When even began to darken to night,
They would hie along in the fading light,

[119]

With elf-locked hair and scarlet lips,
And small stone knives to slit the skeps,
So softly not a bee inside
Should hear the woven straw divide.
And then with sly and greedy thumbs
Would rifle the sweet honeycombs.
And drowsily drone to drone would say,
" A cold, cold wind blows in this way ";
And the great Queen would turn her head
From face to face, astonishèd,
And, though her maids with comb and brush
Would comb and soothe and whisper, " Hush! "
About the hive would shrilly go
A-keeening — keening, to and fro;
At which those robbers 'neath the trees
Would taunt and mock the honey-bees,
And through their sticky teeth would buzz
Just as an angry hornet does.
And when this Gimmul and this Mell
Had munched and sucked and swilled their fill,
Or ever Man's first cock should crow
Back to their Faërie Mounds they'd go.
Edging across the twilight air,
Thieves of a guise remotely fair.

THE THREE BEGGARS

'Twas autumn daybreak gold and wild
    While past St. Ann's grey tower they shuffled
Three beggars spied a fairy-child
    In crimson mantle muffled.

The daybreak lighted up her face
    All pink, and sharp, and emerald-eyed;
She looked on them a little space,
        And shrill as hautboy cried: —

" O three tall footsore men in rags
  Which walking this gold morn I see,
What will ye give me from your bags
  For fairy kisses three ? "

The first, that was a reddish man,
  Out of his bundle takes a crust:
" La, by the tombstones of St. Ann
  There's fee, if fee ye must ! "

The second, that was a chestnut man,
  Out of his bundle draws a bone:
" La, by the belfry of St. Ann,
  And all my breakfast gone ! "

The third, that was a yellow man,
  Out of his bundle picks a groat,
" La, by the Angel of St. Ann,
  And I must go without."

That changeling, lean and icy-lipped,
  Touched crust, and bone, and groat, and lo!
Beneath her finger taper-tipped
  The magic all ran through.

Instead of crust a peacock pie,
  Instead of bone sweet venison,
Instead of groat a white lily
  With seven blooms thereon.

And each fair cup was deep with wine:
  Such was the changeling's charity
The sweet feast was enough for nine,
  But not too much for three.

O toothsome meat in jelly froze!
  O tender haunch of elfin stag!
Oh, rich the odour that arose!
  Oh, plump with scraps each bag!

There, in the daybreak gold and wild,
  Each merry-hearted beggarman
Drank deep unto the fairy child,
  And blessed the good St. Ann.

BERRIES

There was an old woman
  Went blackberry picking
Along the hedges
  From Weep to Wicking.

Half a pottle —
  No more she had got,
When out steps a Fairy
  From her green grot;

And says, " Well, Jill,
    Would 'ee pick 'ee mo ? "
And Jill, she curtseys,
    And looks just so.
" Be off," says the Fairy,
    " As quick as you can,
Over the meadows
    To the little green lane,
That dips to the hayfields
    Of Farmer Grimes:
I've berried those hedges
    A score of times;
Bushel on bushel
    I'll promise 'ee, Jill,
This side of supper
    If 'ee pick with a will."
She glints very bright,
    And speaks her fair;
Then lo, and behold!
    She had faded in air.

Be sure Old Goodie
    She trots betimes
Over the meadows
    To Farmer Grimes.
And never was queen
    With jewellery rich
As those same hedges
    From twig to ditch;
Like Dutchmen's coffers,
    Fruit, thorn, and flower —
They shone like William
    And Mary's bower.

And be sure Old Goodie
    Went back to Weep
So tired with her basket
    She scarce could creep.

When she comes in the dusk
    To her cottage door,
There's Towser wagging
    As never before,
To see his Missus
    So glad to be
Come from her fruit-picking
    Back to he.
As soon as next morning
    Dawn was grey,
The pot on the hob
    Was simmering away;
And all in a stew
    And a hugger-mugger
Towser and Jill
    A-boiling of sugar,
And the dark clear fruit
    That from Faërie came,
For syrup and jelly
    And blackberry jam.

Twelve jolly gallipots
    Jill put by;
And one little teeny one,
    One inch high;
And that she's hidden
    A good thumb deep,
Halfway over
    From Wicking to Weep.

THE DWARF

" Now, Jinnie, my dear, to the dwarf be off,
    That lives in Barberry Wood,
And fetch me some 'honey, but be sure you don't laugh, —
    He hates little girls that are rude, are rude,
        He hates little girls that are rude."

Jane tapped at the door of the house in the wood,
    And the dwarf looked over the wall,
He eyed her so queer, 'twas as much as she could
    To keep from laughing at all, at all,
        To keep from laughing at all.

His shoes down the passage came clod, clod, clod,
    And when he opened the door,
He croaked so harsh, 'twas as much as she could
    To keep from laughing the more, the more,
        To keep from laughing the more.

As there, with his bushy red beard, he stood
    Pricked out to double its size,
He squinted so cross, 'twas as much as she could
    To keep the tears out of her eyes, her eyes,
        To keep the tears out of her eyes.

He slammed the door, and went clod, clod, clod,
    But while in the porch she bides,
He squealed so fierce, 'twas as much as she could
    To keep from cracking her sides, her sides,
        To keep from cracking her sides.

He threw a pumpkin over the wall,
    And melons and apples beside,
So thick in the air that to see 'em all fall,
    She laughed, and laughed, till she cried, cried, cried,
        Jane laughed and laughed till she cried.

Down fell her teardrops a pit-apat-pat,
    And red as a rose she grew; —
" Kah! kah!" said the dwarf, " is it crying you're at?
    It's the very worst thing you could do, do, do,
        It's the very worst thing you could do."

He slipped like a monkey up into a tree,
    He shook her down cherries like rain;
" See now," says he, cheeping, " a blackbird I be,
    Laugh, laugh, little Jinnie, again-gain-gain!"
        Laugh, laugh, little Jinnie, again. "

Ah me! what a strange, what a gladsome duet
    From a house in the deeps of a wood!
Such shrill and such harsh voices never met yet
    A-laughing as loud as they could, could, could,
        A-laughing as loud as they could.

Come Jinnie, come dwarf, cocksparrow, and bee,
    There's a ring gaudy-green in the dell,
Sing, sing, ye sweet cherubs, that flit in the tree;
    La! who can draw tears from a well, well, well,
        Who ever drew tears from a well!

HAPLESS

Hapless, hapless, I must be
All the hours of life I see,
Since my foolish nurse did once
Bed me on her leggen bones;
Since my mother did not weel
To snip my nails with blades of steel.
Had they laid me on a pillow
In a cot of water willow,
Had they bitten finger and thumb,
Not to such ill hap I had come.

PEAK AND PUKE

From his cradle in the glamourie
They have stolen my wee brother,
Housed a changeling in his swaddlings
For to fret my own poor mother.
Pules it in the candlelight
Wi' a cheek so lean and white,
Chinkling up its eyne so wee
Wailing shrill at her an' me.
It we'll neither rock nor tend
Till the Silent Silent send,
Lapping in their waesome arms
Him they stole with spells and charms,
Till they take this changeling creature
Back to its own fairy nature —
Cry! Cry! as long as may be,
Ye shall ne'er be woman's baby!

THE FAIRY-PEDLAR'S SONG
(From *Crossings*)

Of your 'nevolent nature
    Spare a crust for a creature.
A drink and a dole,
    For a ho-omeless soul.

Of slumber but tossings —
    White the rime in bare Crossings;
Cold is shed, barn and byre, leddy,
    A coal from your fire, leddy!

And Oh, sleepy odours,
    The bosom to lull;
When the swart raven yells,
    And the taper burns dull!

[126]

SOLITUDE

" Wish! and it's thine! " the changeling piped,
 Shrill from her thorn.
And I with dew-soaked shoes could only
 Stare in return.

High up above me sang the lark,
 Beneath me lay the sea,
Gorse, bramble, rock and whinchat were
 My only company.

Her tiny voice fell faint, and lo,
 Where she had been
Leaned but a few-days-budded rose
 Out of the green.

THE RUIN

When the last colours of the day
Have from their burning ebbed away,
About that ruin, cold and lone,
The cricket shrills from stone to stone;
And scattering o'er its darkened green,
Bands of the fairies may be seen,
Chattering like grasshoppers, their feet
Dancing a thistledown dance round it:
While the great gold of the mild moon
Tinges their tiny acorn shoon.

NEVER

" Take me, or leave me — I'm not thine,"
The fairy mocked on the sands of Lyne —

Frail as Phosphor over the sea:
" Seven long years shalt thou toil for me."

Full seven I laboured, teen and tine:
But — " Take me, or leave me, I'm not thine! "

THE BIRD

As poor old Biddie
Sat by the hearth
Chilled to the bone
By the cold in the earth,
Under the eaves —
Biddie nodding and napping —
Came a beak at the casement,
Tap — tapping — and tapping:
Dark creeping in,
The fields all thick
With hoar-frost — still tapping
That restless beak.
But Biddie, as deaf
As a post, drowsed on;
And at last in the starlight
The tapping was gone.
Three mortal days
Lagged wintrily through,
But at midnight on Thursday
Gone was old Biddie too.

DAME HICKORY

" Dame Hickory, Dame Hickory,
Here's sticks for your fire,
Furze-twigs, and oak-twigs,
And beech-twigs, and brier! "
But when old Dame Hickory came for to see,
She found 'twas the voice of the False Faërie.

" Dame Hickory, Dame Hickory,
Here's meat for your broth,
Goose-flesh, and hare's flesh,
And pig's trotters both! "
But when old Dame Hickory came for to see,
She found 'twas the voice of the False Faërie.

" Dame Hickory, Dame Hickory,
Here's a wolf at your door,
His teeth grinning white,
And his tongue wagging sore! "
" Nay! " said Dame Hickory, " ye False Faërie! "
But a wolf 'twas indeed, and famished was he.

" Dame Hickory, Dame Hickory,
Here's buds for your tomb,
Bramble, and lavender,
And rosemary bloom! "
" Whsst! " sighs Dame Hickory, " you False Faërie,
You cry like a wolf, you do, and trouble poor me."

THE MOCKING FAIRY

" Won't you look out of your window, Mrs. Gill? "
    Quoth the Fairy, nidding, nodding in the garden;
" *Can't* you look out of your window, Mrs. Gill? "
    Quoth the Fairy, laughing softly in the garden;

But the air was still, the cherry boughs were still,
And the ivy-tod 'neath the empty sill,
And never from her window looked out Mrs. Gill
    On the Fairy shrilly mocking in the garden.

" What have they done with you, you poor Mrs. Gill? "
    Quoth the Fairy brightly glancing in the garden;
" Where have they hidden you, you poor old Mrs. Gill? "
    Quoth the Fairy dancing lightly in the garden;
But night's faint veil now wrapped the hill,
Stark 'neath the stars stood the dead-still Mill,
And out of her cold cottage never answered Mrs. Gill
    The Fairy mimbling, mambling in the garden.

THE PEDLAR

There came a Pedlar to an evening house;
Sweet Lettice, from her lattice looking down,
Wondered what man he was, so curious
His black hair dangled on his tattered gown:
Then lifts he up his face, with glittering eyes, —
" What will you buy, sweetheart? — Here's honeycomb,
And mottled pippins, and sweet mulberry pies,
Comfits and peaches, snowy cherry bloom,
To keep in water for to make night sweet:
All that you want, sweetheart, — come, taste and eat! "

Ev'n with his sugared words, returned to her
The clear remembrance of a gentle voice: —
" And Oh, my child, should ever a flatterer
Tap with his wares, and promise of all joys
And vain sweet pleasures that on earth may be;
Seal up your ears, sing some old happy song,
Confuse his magic who is all mockery:
His sweets are death." Yet, still, how she doth long
But just to taste, then shut the lattice tight,
And hide her eyes from the delicious sight!

[130]

"What must I pay?" she whispered. "Pay!" says he,
"Pedlar I am who through this wood do roam,
One lock of hair is gold enough for me,
For apple, peach, comfits, or honeycomb!"
But from her bough a drowsy squirrel cried,
"Trust him not, Lettice, trust, oh trust him not!"
And many another woodland tongue beside
Rose softly in the silence — "Trust him not!"
Then cried the Pedlar in a bitter voice,
"What, in the thicket, is this idle noise?"

A late, harsh blackbird smote him with her wings,
As through the glade, dark in the dim, she flew;
Yet still the Pedlar his old burden sings, —
"What, pretty sweetheart, shall I show to you?"

Here's orange ribands, here's a string of pearls,
Here's silk of buttercup and pansy glove,
A pin of tortoise-shell for windy curls,
A box of silver, scented sweet with clove:
Come now," he says, with dim and lifted face,
" I pass not often such a lonely place."

" Pluck not a hair! " a hidden rabbit cried,
" With but one hair he'll steal thy heart away,
Then only sorrow shall your lattice hide:
Go in! all honest pedlars come by day."
There was dead silence in the drowsy wood;
" Here's syrup for to lull sweet maids to sleep;
And bells for dreams, and fairy wine and food
All day your heart in happiness to keep "; —
And now she takes the scissors on her thumb, —
" O, then, no more unto my lattice come! "

Oh, sad the sound of weeping in the wood!
Now only night is where the Pedlar was;
And bleak as frost upon a quickling bud
His magic steals in darkness, O alas!
Why all the summer doth sweet Lettice pine?
And, ere the wheat is ripe, why lies her gold
Hid 'neath fresh new-pluckt sprigs of eglantine?
Why all the morning hath the cuckoo tolled
Sad to and fro in green and secret ways,
With solemn bells the burden of her days?

And, in the market-place, what man is this
Who wears a loop of gold upon his breast,
Stuck heartwise; and whose glassy flatteries
Take all the townfolk ere they go to rest
Who come to buy and gossip? Doth his eye
Remember a face lovely in a wood?
O people! hasten, hasten, do not buy
His woeful wares; the bird of grief doth brood
There where his heart should be; and far away
Dew lies on grave-flowers this selfsame day.

THE OLD HOUSE

A very, very old house I know —
And ever so many people go,
Past the small lodge, forlorn and still,
Under the heavy branches, till
Comes the blank wall, and there's the door.
Go in they do; come out no more.
No voice says aught; no spark of light
Across that threshold cheers the sight;
Only the evening star on high
Less lonely makes a lonely sky,
As, one by one, the people go
Into that very old house I know.

HERE TODAY

Here today and gone tomorrow;
Nowt to buy with, nowt to borrow;
Come the nightshine, packs down all;
Ring poor Robin's funeral.

LONE

Shrill rang the squeak in the empty house
Of the sharp-nosed mouse, the hungry mouse.

" Sing, sing: here none doth dwell! "
Dripped the water in the well.

A robin on the shepherd's grave
Whistled a solitary stave.

And, " Lone-lone! " the curlew cried,
Scolding the sheep-strewn mountain's side.

[133]

As I went to the well-head   " Leagues o'er the water
I heard a bird sing: Their shores are away,
" Lie yonder, lie yonder   In a darkness of stars,
The Islands of Ling.   And a foaming of spray."

ALULVAN

The sun is clear of bird and cloud,
The grass shines windless, grey, and still,
In dusky ruin the owl dreams on,
The cuckoo echoes on the hill;
     Yet soft along Alulvan's walks
       The ghost at noonday stalks.

His eyes in shadow of his hat
Stare on the ruins of his house;
His cloak, up-fastened with a brooch,
Of faded velvet, grey as mouse,
     Brushes the roses as he goes:
       Yet wavers not one rose.

The wild birds in a cloud fly up
From their sweet feeding in the fruit;
The droning of the bees and flies
Rises gradual as a lute;
     Is it for fear the birds are flown,
       And shrills the insect-drone?

Thick is the ivy o'er Alulvan,
And crisp with summer-heat its turf;
For, far across its empty pastures
Alulvan's sands are white with surf:
     And he himself is grey as the sea,
       Watching beneath an elder-tree.

All night the fretful, shrill Banshee
Lurks in the chambers' dark festoons,
Calling for ever, o'er garden and river,
Through magpie changing of the moons:
    " Alulvan, O, alas! Alulvan,
        The doom of lone Alulvan! "

THE LITTLE GREEN ORCHARD

Some one is always sitting there,
        In the little green orchard;
   Even when the sun is high,
   In noon's unclouded sky,
   And faintly droning goes
   The bee from rose to rose,
Some one in shadow is sitting there,
        In the little green orchard.

Yes, and when twilight's falling softly
        On the little green orchard;
   When the grey dew distils
   And every flower-cup fills;
   When the last blackbird says,
   " What — what! " and goes her way — ssh!
I have heard voices calling softly
        In the little green orchard.

Not that I am afraid of being there,
        In the little green orchard;
   Why, when the moon's been bright,
   Shedding her lonesome light,
   And moths like ghosties come,
   And the horned snail leaves home:
I've sat there, whispering and listening there,
        In the little green orchard;

Only it's strange to be feeling there,
   In the little green orchard;
Whether you paint or draw,
Dig, hammer, chop, or saw;
When you are most alone.
All but the silence gone . . .
Some one is waiting and watching there,
   In the little green orchard.

THE VOICE

As I sat in the gloaming
I heard a voice say,
Weep no more, sigh no more;
Come, come away!

It was dusk at the window;
From down in the street
No rumble of carts came,
No passing of feet.

I sat very still,
Too frightened to play;

And again the voice called me,
Little boy, come away!

Dark, darker it grew;
Stars came out, and the moon
Shone clear through the glass
The carpet upon.

I listened and listened;
But no more would it say —
The voice that had called me,
Come, come away!

SORCERY

" What voice is that I hear
  Crying across the pool ? "
" It is the voice of Pan you hear,
Crying his sorceries shrill and clear,
  In the twilight dim and cool."

" What song is it he sings,
  Echoing from afar;
While the sweet swallow bends her wings,
Filling the air with twitterings,
  Beneath the brightening star ? "

[136]

The woodman answered me,
His faggot on his back: —
" Seek not the face of Pan to see;
Flee from his clear note summoning thee
To darkness deep and black!

" He dwells in thickest shade,
Piping his notes forlorn
Of sorrow never to be allayed;
Turn from his coverts sad
Of twilight unto morn! "

The woodman passed away
Along the forest path;
His axe shone keen and grey
In the last beams of day:
And all was still as death: —

Only Pan singing sweet
Out of Earth's fragrant shade;
I dreamed his eyes to meet,
And found but shadow laid
Before my tired feet.

Comes no more dawn to me,
Nor bird of open skies.
Only his woods' deep gloom I see
Till, at the end of all, shall rise,
Afar and tranquilly,
Death's stretching sea.

THE STRANGER

In the nook of a wood where a pool freshed with dew
Glassed, daybreak till evening, blue sky glimpsing through,
Then a star; or a slip of May-moon silver-white
Thridding softly aloof the quiet of night,
Was a thicket of flowers.

Willow-herb, mint, pale speedwell and rattle,
Water hemlock and sundew — to the wind's tittle-tattle
They nodded, dreamed, swayed in jocund delight,
In beauty and sweetness arrayed, still and bright.
By turn scampered rabbit; trotted fox; bee and bird
Paused droning, sang shrill, and the fair water stirred.
Plashed green frog, or some brisk little flickering fish —
Gudgeon, stickleback, minnow — set the ripples a-swish.

A lone pool, a pool grass-fringed, crystal-clear:
Deep, placid, and cool in the sweet of the year;
Edge-parched when the sun to the Dog Days drew near;
And with winter's bleak rime hard as glass, robed in snow,
The whole wild-wood sleeping, and nothing a-blow
But the wind from the North — bringing snow.

That is all. Save that one long, sweet, June night-tide straying,
The harsh hemlock's pale umbelliferous bloom
Tenting nook, dense with fragrance and secret with gloom,
In a beaming of moon-coloured light faintly raying,
On buds orbed with dew phosphorescently playing,
Came a Stranger — still-footed, feat-fingered, clear face,
Unhumanly lovely . . . and supped in that place.

THE STRANGER

A little after twilight,
When the Bear was high in heaven,
And Venus in her beauty
Stood shining in the even;
Still and hushed was the dell
And she came like a flame —
A Stranger, clad in cramoisy,
And danced in the same.

Dew wells not more quietly,
More softly doth shine,
She danced till her cheek
Was red as red wine,
Light like a little taper
Burned small in her eye;
Like snow, like waterdrops, her feet
Twirled softly by.

Not a sound. Not a bird
Stirred a soft folded wing,
While deep in the woodland
She only did sing
Who hath night for her arbour,
For playmate the moon,
And a brook for babbling music there,
Murmuring alone.

Hours scattered their dust,
Night wanned and drew on
A veil of pale silver,
And lo, it was dawn!
Green, green glowed the dell,
And the leaves over, green:
But where was She in cramoisy
Who'd danced in the same?

HAUNTED

From out the wood I watched them shine, —
    The windows of the haunted house,
Now ruddy as enchanted wine,
    Now dark as flittermouse.

There went a thin voice piping airs
    Along the grey and crooked walks, —
A garden of thistledown and tares,
    Bright leaves, and giant stalks.

[139]

The twilight rain shone at its gates,
    Where long-leaved grass in shadow grew;
And back in silence to her mates
    A voiceless raven flew.

Lichen and moss the lone stones greened,
    Green paths led lightly to its door,
Keen from her lair the spider leaned,
    And dusk to darkness wore.

  Amidst the sedge a whisper ran,
    The West shut down a heavy eye,
And like last tapers, few and wan,
    The watch-stars kindled in the sky.

THE ENCHANTED HILL

From height of noon, remote and still,
The sun shines on the empty hill.
No mist, no wind, above, below;
No living thing strays to and fro.
No bird replies to bird on high,
Cleaving the skies with echoing cry.
Like dreaming water, green and wan,
Glassing the snow of mantling swan,
Like a clear jewel encharactered
With secret symbol of line and word,
Asheen, unruffled, slumbrous, still,
The sunlight streams on the empty hill.

But soon as Night's dark shadows ride
Across its shrouded Eastern side,
When at her kindling, clear and full,
Star beyond star stands visible;
Then course pale phantoms, fleet-foot deer
Lap of its waters icy-clear.
Mounts the large moon, and pours her beams
On bright-fish-flashing, singing streams.

Voices re-echo. Coursing by,
Horsemen, like clouds, wheel silently.
Glide then from out their pitch-black lair
Beneath the dark's ensilvered arch,
Witches becowled into the air;
And iron pine and emerald larch,
Tents of delight for ravished bird,
Are by loud music thrilled and stirred.
Winging the light, with silver feet,
Beneath their bowers of fragrance met,
In dells of rose and meadowsweet,
In mazy dance the fairies flit;
While drives his share the Ploughman high
Athwart the daisy-powdered sky:
Till far away, in thickening dew,
Piercing the Eastern shadows through,
Rilling in crystal clear and still,
Light 'gins to tremble on the hill.
And like a mist on faint winds borne,
Silent, forlorn, wells up the morn.
Then the broad sun with burning beams
Steeps slope and peak and gilded streams.
Then no foot stirs; the brake shakes not;
Soundless and wet in its green grot
As if asleep, the leaf hangs limp;
The white dews drip untrembling down,
From bough to bough, orblike, unblown;
And in strange quiet, shimmering and still.
Morning enshrines the empty hill.

WILL-O'-THE-WISP

" Will-o'-the-Wisp,
Come out of the fen,
And vex no more
Benighted men! "

Pale, blue,
Wavering, wan,
" Will-o'-the-Wisp,
Begone, begone! "

[141]

But the trees weep,
The mist-drops hang,
Light dwindles
The bents among.

Oh, and he hovers,
Oh, and he flies,
Will-o'-the-Wisp,
With the baleful eyes.

SOME ONE

Some one came knocking
    At my wee, small door;
Some one came knocking,
    I'm sure — sure — sure;
I listened, I opened,
    I looked to left and right,
But nought there was a-stirring
    In the still dark night;

Only the busy beetle
    Tap-tapping in the wall,
Only from the forest
    The screech-owl's call,
Only the cricket whistling
    While the dewdrops fall,
So I know not who came knock-
    ing,
    At all, at all, at all.

AT THE KEYHOLE

" Grill me some bones," said the Cobbler,
    " Some bones, my pretty Sue;
I'm tired of my lonesome with heels and soles,
Springsides and uppers too;
A mouse in the wainscot is nibbling;
A wind in the keyhole drones;
And a sheet webbed over my candle, Susie, —
    Grill me some bones! "

" Grill me some bones," said the Cobbler,
    " I sat at my tic-tac-to;
And a footstep came to my door and stopped,
And a hand groped to and fro;
And I peered up over my boot and last;
And my feet went cold as stones: —
I saw an eye at the keyhole, Susie! —
    Grill me some bones! "

THE OLD TAILOR

There was once an old Tailor of Hickery Mo,
Too tired at evening to sew, to sew;
He put by his needle, he snapped his thread,
And, cross-legged, sang to his fiddle instead.
His candle bobbed at each note that came
And spat out a spark from the midst of its flame;
His catgut strings they yelped and yawled,
The wilder their scrapings the louder he bawled;
The grease trickled over at every beat,
Welled down to the stick in a winding-sheet —
Till up sprang Puss from the fire, with a *WOW!*
" A *fine* kakkamangul you're making now! "

NOTHING

Whsst, and away, and over the green,
Scampered a shape that never was seen.
It ran without sound, it ran without shadow,
Never a grass-blade in unmown meadow
Stooped at the thistledown fall of its foot.
I watched it vanish, yet saw it not —
A moment past, it had gazed at me;
Now nought but myself and the spindle tree.
A nothing! — Of air? Of earth? Of sun? —
From emptiness come, into vacancy gone! . . .
Whsst, and away, and over the green,
Scampered a shape that never was seen.

THE PHANTOM

" Upstairs in the large closet, child,
    This side the blue-room door,
Is an old Bible, bound in leather,
    Standing upon the floor.

" Go with this taper, bring it me;
    Carry it on your arm;
It is the book on many a sea
    Hath stilled the waves' alarm! "

Late the hour; dark the night;
    The house is solitary;
Feeble is a taper's light
    To light poor Ann to see.

[144]

Her eyes are yet with visions bright
   Of sylph and river, flower and fay,
Now through a narrow corridor
   She goes her lonely way.

Vast shadows on the heedless walls
   Gigantic loom, stoop low:
Each little hasty footfall calls
   Hollowly to and fro.

Now in the dark clear glass there moves
   A taper, mocking hers, —
A phantom face of light blue eyes,
   Reflecting phantom fears.

Around her loom the vacant rooms,
   Wind the upward stairs,
She climbs on into a loneliness
   Only her taper shares.

Out in the dark a cold wind stirs,
   At every window sighs;
A waning moon peers small and chill
   From out the cloudy skies,

Casting faint tracery on the walls;
   So stony still the house
From cellar to attic rings the shrill
   Squeak of the hungry mouse.

Ann scarce can hear or breathe, so fast
   Her pent-up heart doth beat,
When, faint along the corridor,
   She hears the fall of feet: —

Sounds lighter than silk slippers make
   Upon a ballroom floor, when sweet
Violin and 'cello wake
   Music for twirling feet.

[145]

O! in an old unfriendly house,
  What shapes may not conceal
Their faces in the open day,
  At night abroad to steal!

Even her taper seems with fear
  To languish small and blue;
Far in the woods the winter wind
  Runs whistling through.

A dreadful cold plucks at each hair,
  Her mouth is stretched to cry,
But sudden, with a gush of joy,
  It narrows to a sigh.

'Tis but a phantom child which comes
  Soft through the corridor,
Singing an old forgotten song,
  This ancient burden bore: —

" Thorn, thorn, I wis,
And roses twain,
  A red rose and a white;
Stoop in the blossom, bee, and kiss
  A lonely child good-night.

" Swim fish, sing bird,
And sigh again,
  I that am lost am lone,
Bee in the blossom never stirred
  Locks hid beneath a stone! " —

Her eyes were of the azure fire
  That hovers in wintry flame;
Her raiment wild and yellow as furze
  That spouteth out the same;

And in her hand she bore no flower,
 But on her head a wreath
Of faded flowers that did yet
 Smell sweetly after death. . . .

Gloomy with night the listening walls
 Are now that she is gone,
Albeit this solitary child
 No longer seems alone.

Fast though her taper dwindles down,
 Though black the shadows come,
A beauty beyond fear to dim
 Haunts now her alien home.

Ghosts in the world, malignant, grim,
 Vex many a wood and glen,
And house and pool, — the unquiet ghosts
 Of dead and restless men.

But in her grannie's house this spirit —
 A child as lone as she —
Pining for love not found on earth,
 Ann dreams again to see.

Seated upon her tapestry-stool,
 Her fairy-book laid by,
She gazes into the fire, knowing
 She hath sweet company.

IN THE DYING OF DAYLIGHT

In the dying of the daylight —
With my book, and alone —
Of a sudden my heart
Paused, still as a stone.

I watched, I listened;
There was nothing to hear;
Yet I knew, in the silence,
Some living thing near.

I crept to the staircase,
And stayed — there to see
A child at the window
Who not yet had seen me.

She had stooped her small
        head,
In the darkening air,
Low over the flowers
In a bowl that was there,

Her chin on their petals;
Her clear, sidelong eyes
Gazing out of the glass
At the light in the skies.

She was not of this earth —
Lost, solitary,
In the stealth of the house
She was sharing with me:

Yet never have I,
Awake, or at night,
Seen in any strange face
So intense a delight;

So hungry a gaze,
Fixed, enraptured and still,
On the green of the grass,
And the light on the hill;

As if parched up with thirst
For the loved that no more
To a heart, lost to earth,
Earth could ever restore.

And yet — when I turned,
But scarcely had stirred,
At a sound, like the note
Of a late evening bird,
Then looked back — she was gone;
As if she, too, had heard.

THE HOUSE

A lane at the end of Old Pilgrim Street
Leads on to a sheep-track over the moor,
Till you come at length to where two streams meet,
The brook called Liss, and the shallow Stour.

Their waters mingle and sing all day —
Rushes and kingcups, rock and stone;
And aloof in the valley, forlorn and grey,
Is a house whence even the birds have flown.

Its ramshackle gate swings crazily; but
No sickle covets its seeding grass;
There's a cobbled path to a door close-shut;
But no face shows at the window-glass.

No smoke wreathes up in the empty air
From the chimney over its weed-green thatch;
Brier and bryony ramble there;
And no thumb tirls at the broken latch.

Even the warbling water seems
To make lone music for none to hear;
Else is a quiet found only in dreams,
And in dreams this foreboding, though not of fear.

Yes, often at dusk-fall when nearing home —
The hour of the crescent and evening star —
Again to the bridge and the streams I come,
Where the sedge and the rushes and kingcups are:

And I stand, and listen, and sigh — in vain;
Since only of Fancy's the face I see;
Yet its eyes, in the twilight on mine remain,
And it seems to be craving for company.

THE OLD STONE HOUSE

Nothing on the grey roof, nothing on the brown,
Only a little greening where the rain drips down;
Nobody at the window, nobody at the door,
Only a little hollow which a foot once wore;
But still I tread on tiptoe, still tiptoe on I go,
Past nettles, porch, and weedy well, for oh, I know
A friendless face is peering, and a clear still eye
Peeps closely through the casement as my step goes by.

CRAZED

I know a pool where nightshade preens
Her poisonous fruitage in the moon;
Where the frail aspen her shadow leans
In midnight cold a-swoon.

I know a meadow flat with gold —
A million million shining flowers
In noon-sun's thirst their buds unfold
Beneath his blazing showers.

I saw a crazèd face, did I,
Stare from the lattice of a mill,
While the lank sails clacked idly by
High on the windy hill.

MISERICORDIA

Misericordia!
Weep with me.
Waneth the dusk light;
Strange the tree;
In regions barbarous
Lost are we

I, Glycera,
And Silas here,
Who hath hid in sleep
His eyes from fear;
Wan-wide are mine
With a tear.

Misericordia!
Was I born
Only to pluck
Disaster's thorn?
Only to stray
Forlorn?

THE TRUANTS

Ere my heart beats too coldly and faintly
  To remember sad things, yet be gay,
I would sing a brief song of the world's little children
  Magic hath stolen away.

The primroses scattered by April,
　　The stars of the wide Milky Way,
Cannot outnumber the hosts of the children
　　Magic hath stolen away.

The buttercup green of the meadows,
　　The snow of the blossoming may,
Lovelier are not than the legions of children
　　Magic hath stolen away.

The waves tossing surf in the moonbeam,
　　The Albatross lone on the spray,
Alone know the tears wept in vain for the children
　　Magic hath stolen away.

In vain: for at hush of the evening,
　　When the stars twinkle into the grey,
Seems to echo the far-away calling of children
　　Magic hath stolen away.

LONGLEGS

Longlegs — he yelled " Coo-ee! "
　　And all across the combe
Shrill and shrill it rang — rang through
　　The clear green gloom.
Fairies there were a-spinning,
　　And a white tree-maid
Lifted her eyes, and listened
　　In her rain-sweet glade.
Bunnie to bunnie stamped; old Wat
　　Chin-deep in bracken sate;
A throstle piped, " I'm by, I'm by! "
　　Clear to his timid mate.
And there was Longlegs straddling,
　　And hearkening was he,
To distant Echo thrilling back
　　A thin " Coo-ee! "

THE OGRE

'Tis moonlight on Trebarwith Sands,
    And moonlight on their seas,
Lone in a cove a cottage stands
    Enclustered in with trees.

Snuffing its thin faint smoke afar
    An Ogre prowls, and he
Smells supper; for where humans are,
    Rich dainties too may be.

Sweet as a larder to a mouse,
    So to him staring down,
Seemed the small-windowed moonlit house,
    With jasmine overgrown.

He snorted, as the billows snort
    In darkness of the night,
Betwixt his lean locks tawny-swart,
    He glowered on the sight.

Into the garden sweet with peas
    He put his wooden shoe,
And bending back the apple trees
    Crept covetously through;

Then, stooping, with an impious eyè
    Stared through the lattice small,
And spied two children which did lie
    Asleep, against the wall.

Into their dreams no shadow fell
    Of his disastrous thumb
Groping discreet, and gradual,
    Across the quiet room.

But scarce his nail had scraped the cot
  Wherein these children lay,
As if his malice were forgot,
  It suddenly did stay.

For faintly in the inglenook
  He heard a cradle-song,
That rose into his thoughts and woke
  Terror them among.

For she who in the kitchen sat
  Darning by the fire,
Guileless of what he would be at,
  Sang sweet as wind or wire: —

"Lullay, thou little tiny child,
  By-by, lullay, lullie;
Jesu in glory, meek and mild,
  This night remember thee!

"Fiend, witch, and goblin, foul and wild,
  He deems them smoke to be;
Lullay, thou little tiny child,
  By-by, lullay, lullie!"

The Ogre lifted up his eyes
  Into the moon's pale ray,
And gazed upon her leopard-wise,
  Cruel and clear as day;

He snarled in gluttony and fear —
  The wind blows dismally —
"Jesu in storm my lambs be near,
  By-by, lullay, lullie!"

And like a ravenous beast which sees
  The hunter's icy eye,
So did this wretch in wrath confess
  Sweet Jesu's mastery.

With gaunt locks dangling, crouched he, then
   Drew backward from his prey,
Through tangled apple-boughs again
   He wrenched and rent his way.

Out on Trebarwith Sands he broke,
   The waves yelled back his cry,
Gannet and cormorant echo woke
   As he went striding by.

JOHN MOULDY

I spied John Mouldy in his cellar,
   Deep down twenty steps of stone;
In the dusk he sat a-smiling,
   Smiling there alone.

He read no book, he snuffed no candle;
   The rats ran in, the rats ran out;
And far and near, the drip of water
   Went whisp'ring about.

The dusk was still, with dew a-falling,
   I saw the Dog Star bleak and grim,
I saw a slim brown rat of Norway.
   Creep over him.

I spied John Mouldy in his cellar,
   Deep down twenty steps of stone;
In the dusk he sat a-smiling,
   Smiling there alone.

THE PILGRIM

" Shall we help you with your bundle,
     You old grey man ?
Over hill and dell and meadow
Lighter than an owlet's shadow
We will waft it through the air,
Through blue regions shrill and bare
So you may in comfort fare —
Shall we help you with your bundle.
     You old grey man ? "

The Pilgrim lifted up his eyes
And saw three Fiends in the skies,
Stooping o'er that lonely place
     Evil in form and face.

" Nay," he answered, " tempt me not,
     O three wild Fiends!
Long the journey I am wending,
Yet the longest hath an ending;
I must bear my bundle alone
     Till the day be done."
The Fiends stared down with leaden eye,
Fanning the chill air duskily,
'Twixt their hoods they stoop and cry: —

" Shall we smooth the path before you,
     Weary old man ?
Sprinkle it green with gilded showers,
Strew it o'er with painted flowers,
Lure bright birds to sing and flit
In the honeyed airs of it ?
Shall we smooth the path before you,
     Sad old man ? "

" O, 'tis better silence,
     Ye three wild Fiends!
Footsore am I, faint and weary,

Dark the way, forlorn and dreary,
Even so, at peace I be,
Nor want for ghostly company:
O, 'tis better silence,
    Ye three wild Fiends! "

It seemed a cloud obscured the air,
Lightning quivered in the gloom,
And a faint voice of thunder spake
Far in the high hill-hollows — " Come! "
Then, half in fury, half in dread,
The Fiends drew closer down, and said:

" Nay, thou foolish fond old man,
    Hearken awhile!
Frozen, scorched, with ice and heat,
Tarry now, sit down and eat:
Juice of purple grape shall be
Joy and solace unto thee.

" Music of tambour, wire and wind,
Ease shall bring to heart and mind;
Wonderful sweet mouths shall sigh
Languishing and lullaby;
Turn then! Curse the dream that lures thee;
Turn thee, ere too late it be,
Lest thy three true Friends grow weary
    Of comforting thee! "

The Pilgrim crouches terrified
At stooping hood, and glassy face,
Gloating, evil, side by side,
Terror and hate brood o'er the place;
He flings his withered hands on high
With a bitter, breaking cry: —

" Pity have, and leave me, leave me,
    Ye three wild Fiends!
If I lay me down in slumber
Dark with death that sleep shall be;

All your fruits are fruits of evil —
Wrath and hate and treachery.
On mine eyes the darkness thickens,
Blind, in dread, I stumble on,
Cheat me not with false beguiling —
    Beseech ye, begone! "

And even as he spake, on high
Arrows of sunlight pierced the sky
Bright streamed the rain. O'er burning snow
From hill to hill a wondrous Bow
Of colour and fire trembled in air,
Painting its heavenly beauty there.
Wild flung each Fiend a batlike hood
Against that flaming light, and stood
Beating the windless rain and then
Rose heavy and slow with cowering head,
Circled in company again,
And into darkness fled.

Marvellous sweet it was to hear
The waters gushing loud and clear;
Marvellous happy it was to be
Alone, and yet not solitary;
Oh, out of terror and dark to come
    In sight of home!

I SAW THREE WITCHES

I saw three witches
That bowed down like barley,
And took to their brooms 'neath a louring sky,
And, mounting a storm-cloud,
Aloft on its margin,
Stood black in the silver as up they did fly.

I saw three witches
That mocked the poor sparrows
They carried in cages of wicker along,
Till a hawk from his eyrie
Swooped down like an arrow,
And smote on the cages, and ended their song.

I saw three witches
That sailed in a shallop
All turning their heads with a truculent smile
Till a bank of green osiers
Concealed their grim faces,
Though I heard them lamenting for many a mile.

I saw three witches
Asleep in a valley,
Their heads in a row, like stones in a flood,
Till the moon, creeping upward,
Looked white through the valley,
And turned them to bushes in bright scarlet bud.

THE WITCH

Weary went the old Witch,
Weary of her pack,
She sat her down by the churchyard wall,
And jerked it off her back.

[158]

The cord brake, yes, the cord brake,
Just where the dead did lie,
And Charms and Spells and Sorceries
Spilled out beneath the sky.

Weary was the old Witch;
She rested her old eyes
From the lantern-fruited yew trees,
And the scarlet of the skies;

And out the dead came stumbling,
From every rift and crack,
Silent as moss, and plundered
The gaping pack.

They wish them, three times over,
Away they skip full soon:
Bat and Mole and Leveret,
Under the rising moon;

Owl and Newt and Nightjar:
They take their shapes and creep
Silent as churchyard lichen,
While she squats asleep.

All of these dead were stirring:
Each unto each did call,
" A Witch, a Witch is sleeping
Under the churchyard wall;

"A Witch, a Witch is sleeping . . ."
The shrillness ebbed away;
And up the way-worn moon clomb bright,
Hard on the track of day.

She shone, high, wan, and silvery;
Day's colours paled and died:
And, save the mute and creeping worm,
Nought else was there beside.

Names may be writ; and mounds rise;
Purporting, Here be bones:
But empty is that church yard
Of all save stones.

Owl and Newt and Nightjar,
Leveret, Bat, and Mole
Haunt and call in the twilight
Where she slept, poor soul.

THE JOURNEY

Heart-sick of his journey was the Wanderer;
    Footsore and parched was he;
And a Witch who long had lurked by the wayside,
    Looked out of sorcery.

" Lift up your eyes, you lonely Wanderer,"
    She peeped from her casement small;
" Here's shelter and quiet to give you rest, young man,
    And apples for thirst withal."

And he looked up out of his sad reverie,
    And saw all the woods in green,
With birds that flitted feathered in the dappling,
    The jewel-bright leaves between.

And he lifted up his face toward her lattice,
    And there, alluring-wise,
Slanting through the silence of the long past,
    Dwelt the still green Witch's eyes.

And vaguely from the hiding-place of memory
    Voices seemed to cry;
" What is the darkness of one brief life-time
    To the deaths thou hast made us die ? "

" Heed not the words of the Enchantress
    Who would us still betray! "
And sad with the echo of their reproaches,
    Doubting, he turned away.

" I may not shelter 'neath your roof, lady,
    Nor in this wood's green shadow seek repose,
Nor will your apples quench the thirst
    A homesick wanderer knows."

" ' Homesick,' forsooth! " she softly mocked him:
    And the beauty in her face
Made in the sunshine pale and trembling
    A stillness in that place.

And he sighed, as if in fear, the young Wanderer,
    Looking to left and to right,
Where the endless narrow road swept onward,
    In the distance lost to sight.

And there fell upon his sense the brier,
    Haunting the air with its breath,
And the faint shrill sweetness of the birds' throats,
    Their tent of leaves beneath.

And there was the Witch, in no wise heeding;
    Her arbour, and fruit-filled dish,
Her pitcher of well-water, and clear damask —
    All that the weary wish.

And the last gold beam across the green world
    Faltered and failed, as he
Remembered his solitude and the dark night's
    Inhospitality.

And he looked upon the Witch with eyes of sorrow
    In the darkening of the day;
And turned him aside into oblivion;
    And the voices died away. . . .

And the Witch stepped down from her casement:
    In the hush of night he heard
The calling and wailing in dewy thicket
    Of bird to hidden bird.

And gloom stole all her burning crimson,
    Remote and faint in space
As stars in gathering shadow of the evening
    Seemed now her phantom face.

And one night's rest shall be a myriad,
    Midst dreams that come and go;
Till heedless fate, unmoved by weakness, bring him
    This same strange by-way through:

To the beauty of earth that fades in ashes,
    The lips of welcome, and the eyes
More beauteous than the feeble shine of Hesper
    Lone in the lightening skies:

Till once again the Witch's guile entreat him;
    But, worn with wisdom, he
Steadfast and cold shall choose the dark night's
    Inhospitality.

THE RIDE-BY-NIGHTS

Up on their brooms the Witches stream,
Crooked and black in the crescent's gleam;
One foot high, and one foot low,
Bearded, cloaked, and cowled, they go.
'Neath Charlie's Wane they twitter and tweet,
And away they swarm 'neath the Dragon's feet,
With a whoop and a flutter they swing and sway,
And surge pell-mell down the Milky Way.

Between the legs of the glittering Chair
They hover and squeak in the empty air.
Then round they swoop past the glimmering Lion
To where Sirius barks behind huge Orion;
Up, then, and over to wheel amain
Under the silver, and home again.

AS LUCY WENT A-WALKING

As Lucy went a-walking one morning cold and fine,
There sate three crows upon a bough, and three times three are
   nine:
Then " O! " said Lucy, in the snow, " it's very plain to see
A witch has been a-walking in the fields in front of me."

Then stept she light and heedfully across the frozen snow,
And plucked a bunch of elder-twigs that near a pool did grow:
And, by and by, she comes to seven shadows in one place
Stretched black by seven poplar-trees against the sun's bright face.

She looks to left, she looks to right, and in the midst she sees
A little pool of water clear and frozen 'neath the trees;
Then down beside its margent in the crusted snow she kneels,
And hears a magic belfry, ringing with sweet bells.

Clear rang the faint far merry peal, then silence on the air,
And icy-still the frozen pool and poplars standing there:
Then, soft, as Lucy turned her head and looked along the snow
She sees a witch — a witch she sees, come frisking to and fro.

Her scarlet, buckled shoes they clicked, her heels a-twinkling high;
With mistletoe her steeple-hat bobbed as she capered by;
But never a dint, or mark, or print, in the whiteness there to see,
Though danced she light, though danced she fast, though danced
   she lissomely.

It seemed 'twas diamonds in the air, or tiny flakes of frost;
It seemed 'twas golden smoke around, or sunbeams lightly tossed;
It seemed an elfin music like to reeds' and warblers' rose:
" Nay! " Lucy said, " it is the wind that through the branches flows."

And as she peeps, and as she peeps, 'tis no more one, but three,
And eye of bat, and downy wing of owl within the tree,
And the bells of that sweet belfry a-pealing as before,
And now it is not three she sees, and now it is not four.

" O! who are ye," sweet Lucy cries, " that in a dreadful ring,
All muffled up in brindled shawls, do caper, frisk, and spring? "
" A witch and witches, one and nine," they straight to her reply,
And look upon her narrowly, with green and needle eye.

Then Lucy sees in clouds of gold sweet cherry-trees upgrow,
And bushes of red roses that bloomed above the snow;
She smells all faint the almond-boughs blowing so wild and fair,
And doves with milky eyes ascend fluttering in the air.

Clear flowers she sees, like tulip buds, go floating by like birds,
With wavering tips that warbled sweetly strange enchanted words;
And as with ropes of amethyst the twigs with lamps were hung,
And clusters of green emeralds like fruit upon them clung.

" O witches nine, yet dreadful nine, O witches three times three!
Whence come these wondrous things that I this Christmas morning
    see?
But straight, as in a clap, when she of " Christmas " says the word,
Here is the snow, and there the sun, but never bloom nor bird;

Nor warbling flame, nor gloaming-rope of amethyst there shows,
Nor bunches of green emeralds, nor belfry, well, and rose,
Nor cloud of gold, nor cherry-tree, nor witch in brindled shawl,
But like a dream which vanishes, so vanished were they all.

When Lucy sees, and only sees three crows upon a bough,
And earthly twigs, and bushes hidden white in driven snow,
Then " O! " said Lucy," three times three are nine — I plainly see
Some witch has been a-walking in the fields in front of me."

THE LITTLE CREATURE

Twinkum, twankum, twirlum and twitch —
My great grandam — She was a Witch.
Mouse in wainscot, Saint in niche —
My great grandam — She was a Witch;
Deadly nightshade flowers in a ditch —
My great grandam — She was a Witch;
Long though the shroud, it grows stitch by stitch —
My great grandam — She was a Witch;
Wean your weakling before you breech —
My great grandam — She was a Witch;
The fattest pig's but a double flitch —
My great grandam — She was a Witch;
Nightjars rattle, owls scritch —
My great grandam — She was a Witch.

Pretty and small,
A mere nothing at all,
Pinned up sharp in the ghost of a shawl,
She'd straddle her down to the kirkyard wall,
And mutter and whisper and call,
And call. . . .

Red blood out and black blood in,
My Nannie says I'm a child of sin.
How did I choose me my witchcraft kin?
Know I as soon as dark's dreams begin
Snared is my heart in a nightmare's gin;
Never from terror I out may win;
So dawn and dusk I pine, peak, thin,
Scarcely knowing t'other from which —
My great grandam — She was a Witch.

BEWITCHED

I have heard a lady this night,
    Lissome and jimp and slim,
Calling me — calling me over the heather,
    'Neath the beech boughs dusk and dim.

I have followed a lady this night,
    Followed her far and lone,
Fox and adder and weasel know
    The ways that we have gone.

I sit at my supper 'mid honest faces,
    And crumble my crust and say
Nought in the long-drawn drawl of the voices
    Talking the hours away.

I'll go to my chamber under the gable,
    And the moon will lift her light
In at my lattice from over the moorland
    Hollow and still and bright.

[167]

And I know she will shine on a lady of witchcraft,
　　Gladness and grief to see,
Who has taken my heart with her nimble fingers,
　　Calls in my dreams to me;

Who has led me a dance by dell and dingle
　　My human soul to win,
Made me a changeling to my own, own mother,
　　A stranger to my kin.

THE CHANGELING

" Ahoy, and ahoy! "
　　'Twixt mocking and merry —
" Ahoy and ahoy, there,
　　Young man of the ferry! "

She stood on the steps
　　In the watery gloom —
That Changeling —" Ahoy,
　　there! "
　　She called him to come.
He came on the green wave,
　　He came on the grey,
Where stooped that sweet lady
　That still summer's day.
He fell in a dream
　　Of her beautiful face,
As she sat on the thwart
　　And smiled in her place.

No echo his oar woke,
　　Float silent did they,
Past low-grazing cattle
　　In the sweet of the hay.
And still in a dream
　　At her beauty sat he,
Drifting stern foremost
　　Down — down to the sea.
Come you, then: call,
　　When the twilight apace
Brings shadow to brood
　　On the loveliest face;
You shall hear o'er the water
　　Ring faint in the grey —
" Ahoy, and ahoy, there! "
　　And tremble away;
" Ahoy, and ahoy! . . .
　　And tremble away.

THE COQUETTE

Yearn thou may'st:
Thou shalt not see
My wasting love
For thee.

Lean thy tresses;
Fair that fruit;
Slim as warbling bird's
Thy throat.

Peep thou then:
Doubt not some swain
Will of thy still decoy
Be fain.

But I? In sooth —
Nay, gaze thy fill!
Scorn thee I must,
And will.

A SONG OF ENCHANTMENT

A Song of Enchantment I sang me there,
In a green — green wood, by waters fair,
Just as the words came up to me
I sang it under the wild-wood tree.

Widdershins turned I, singing it low,
Watching the wild birds come and go;
No cloud in the deep dark blue to be seen
Under the thick-thatched branches green.

Twilight came; silence came;
The planet of evening's silver flame;
By darkening paths I wandered through
Thickets trembling with drops of dew.

But the music is lost and the words are gone
Of the song I sang as I sat alone,
Ages and ages have fallen on me —
On the wood and the pool and the elder tree.

NOW SILENT FALLS

Now silent falls the clacking mill;
Sweet — sweeter smells the brier;
The dew wells big on bud and twig;
The glow-worm's wrapt in fire.

Then sing, lully, lullay, with me,
And softly, lill-lall-lo, love,
'Tis high time, and wild time,
And no time, no, love!

The Western sky has vailed her rose;
The night-wind to the willow
Sigheth, " Now, lovely, lean thy head,
Thy tresses be my pillow! "

Then sing, lully, lullay, with me,
And softly, lill-lall-lo, love,
'Tis high time, and wild time,
And no time, no, love!

Cries in the brake, bells in the sea:
The moon o'er moor and mountain
Cruddles her light from height to height,
Bedazzles pool and fountain.

Leap, fox; hoot, owl; wail, warbler sweet:
'Tis midnight now's a-brewing:
The fairy mob is all abroad,
And witches at their wooing . . .

Then sing, lully, lullay, with me,
And softly, lill-lall-lo, love,
'Tis high time, and wild time,
And no time, no, love.

MELMILLO

Three and thirty birds there stood
In an elder in a wood;
Called Melmillo — flew off three,
Leaving thirty in the tree;
Called Melmillo — nine now gone,
And the boughs held twenty-one;
Called Melmillo — and eighteen
Left but three to nod and preen;
Called Melmillo — three — two — one
Now of birds were feathers none.

Then stole slim Melmillo in
To that wood all dusk and green,
And with lean long palms outspread
Softly a strange dance did tread;
Not a note of music she
Had for echoing company;
All the birds were flown to rest
In the hollow of her breast;
In the wood — thorn, elder, willow —
Danced alone — lone danced Melmillo.

QUEEN DJENIRA

When Queen Djenira slumbers through
    The sultry noon's repose,
From out her dreams, as soft she lies,
    A faint thin music flows.

Her lovely hands lie narrow and pale
    With gilded nails, her head
Couched in its banded nets of gold
    Lies pillowed on her bed.

The little Nubian boys who fan
    Her cheeks and tresses clear,
Wonderful, wonderful, wonderful voices
    Seem afar to hear.

They slide their eyes, and nodding, say,
    " Queen Djenira walks today
The courts of the lord Pthamasar
    Where the sweet birds of Psuthys are."

And those of earth about her porch
    Of shadow cool and grey
Their sidelong beaks in silence lean,
    And silent flit away.

THE PHANTOM

Wilt thou never come again,
    Beauteous one?
Yet the woods are green and dim,
Yet the birds' deluding cry
Echoes in the hollow sky,
Yet the falling waters brim
The clear pool which thou wast fain
To paint thy lovely cheek upon,
    Beauteous one!

I may see the thorny rose
    Stir and wake
The dark dewdrop on her gold;
But thy secret will she keep
Half-divulged — yet all untold,
Since a child's heart woke from sleep.
The faltering sunbeam fades and goes;

The night-bird whistles in the brake;
    The willows quake;

Utter quiet falls; the wind
    Sighs no more.
Yet it seems the silence yearns
But to catch thy fleeting foot;
Yet the wandering glow-worm burns
Lest her lamp should light thee not —
Thee whom I shall never find;
Though thy shadow lean before,
Thou thyself return'st no more —
    Never more.

All the world's woods, tree o'er tree,
    Come to nought.
Birds, flowers, beasts, how transient they,
Angels of a flying day.
Love is quenched; dreams drown in sleep;
Ruin nods along the deep:
Only thou immortally
    Hauntest on
This poor earth in Time's flux caught;
Hauntest on, pursued, unwon,
Phantom child of memory,
    Beauteous one!

Winter and
Christmas

BLAISDELL

WHITE

Once a Miller, and he would say,
" I go as *white* as lambs in May!
I go as white as rose on bush!
White as the white convolvulus! "

He snapped his fingers, began to sing: —
" White, by my beard, is everything!
Meal, and chalk, and frost, and hail;
Clouds and surf and ships in sail.

" There's nowt on earth that brighter shines
Than daisies, pinks and columbines;
But what of *ME* when full moon doth show
And mill and meadows are deep in snow! "

SNOW

No breath of wind,
No gleam of sun —
Still the white snow
Whirls softly down —
Twig and bough
And blade and thorn
All in an icy
Quiet, forlorn.
Whispering, rustling,
Through the air,
On sill and stone,
Roof — everywhere,

It heaps its powdery
Crystal flakes,
Of every tree
A mountain makes;
Till pale and faint
At shut of day,
Stoops from the West
One wintry ray.
And, feathered in fire,
Where ghosts the moon,
A robin thrills
His lonely tune.

THE SNOW-MAN

What shape is this in cowl of snow?
    Stiff broom and icy hat?
A saffron moon, half-hidden, stares —
    But what is she staring *at?*

The knocker dangles on the door,
    But stark as tree and post
He blankly eyes the bright green paint,
    Is silent as a ghost.

But wait till belfry midnight strike,
    And up to the stars is tossed
Shrill cockcrow! — *then,* he'll gadding go —
    And, at his heels, Jack Frost:

Broom over shoulder, away he'll go,
Finger-tips tingling, nose aglow,
Dancing and yodelling through the snow,
    And, at his heels, Jack Frost!

THE LITTLE SALAMANDER
To Margot

When I go free,
I think 'twill be
A night of stars and snow,
And the wild fires of frost shall light
My footsteps as I go;
Nobody — nobody will be there
With groping touch, or sight,
To see me in my bush of hair
Dance burning through the night.

THE FIRE

Loud roared the flames
On Bonner's heath,
But all was crudded
Snow beneath,

Save where in shadow,
Clip — clop — clupp,
He stumbled down
Who had stolen up.

LOGS

This tree, by April wreathed in flowers,
That sheened with leaves the summer hours,
    In dappling shine and shade,
Now all that then was lovely lacks,
Is vanquished by the saw and axe,
    And into firewood made.

How happy and gentle a daybreak song
Whispered its solemn boughs among,
    At sigh of morning stirred;
It braved the dangerous lightning; rose
In splendour, crowned with winter's snows;

And sheltered every bird
That perched with slender claw and wing
To preen, to rest, to roost, to sing,
      Unseen — but not unheard.

But came the Woodman with his axe
      Into the sun-sweet glade;
And what was once all beauty and grace
      Is into firewood made.

CAW

Ho, ho, ho, ho!
Now old Winter's winds do blow!
Driving down his flocks of snow.
All the fields where daisies were
He has frozen bleak and bare;
Every bush and hedge he decks
With a myriad shining flakes.
Waiting for the sun to rise,
They stand up like hills of ice;
Glisten, gleam, and flame and burn
Every dazzling hue in turn.
Now the farmer's boy he goes,
Scarlet ears, and redder nose,
Whistling as he shuffles by —
A sea of white, a cloudless sky.
Now the hare peeps out to see
What strange wonder this can be;
And the solemn-headed rook,
Perched above his hooded oak,
Hoarsely caws, and shakes the snow
From his sooty wing; and *" Caw! "*
Cries again: " What have we here,
      Neighbours dear!
The Magician, in one night,
Has changed a world that's green to white! "

CRUMBS

You little birds, I bring my crumbs,
For now the cold of winter comes.
The North Wind blows down frozen rain;
The fields are white with snow again;
The worm's in house; the bare-twigged trees
Are thick with frost instead of bees;
From running brooks all noise is gone;
And every pool lies still as stone.

THE GHOST CHASE

What sight is this? . . . on dazzling snow,
Cold as a shroud beneath the sky,
Swoop into view, the valley through,
Fox, horsemen, hounds — in soundless cry!
   Hullà! Hullo! Hulla-hoo!

Reynard himself, muzzle to brush,
Is whiter than the crystal track
He races over in the hush
Of woods that cast no rumour back.

The voiceless hounds are white as he;
Huntsman and horse — no scarlet theirs;
No fleck, mark, dapple, or spot to see,
White as the North — horses and mares.

They move as in a dream — no stir,
No hoof-fall, music, tongue or steel —
Swift as a noiseless scimitar
Cutting the snows the winds congeal.

Now they are gone. O dove-white yews!
O sleep-still vale! All silent lies
The calm savanna of the snows,
Beneath the blue of arctic skies!
   Hullà! Hullo! Hulla-hoo!

THE HUNTSMEN

Three jolly gentlemen,
        In coats of red,
Rode their horses
        Up to bed.

Three jolly gentlemen
        Snored till morn,
Their horses champing
        The golden corn.

Three jolly gentlemen,
        At break of day,
Came clitter-clatter down the stairs
        And galloped away.

THE SUPPER

A Wolf he pricks with eyes of fire
Across the dark, frost-crusted snows,
        Seeking his prey,
        He pads his way
Where Jane benighted goes,
        Where Jane benighted goes.

He curdles the bleak air with ire,
Ruffling his hoary raiment through,
        And lo! he sees
        Beneath the trees
Where Jane's light footprints go,
        Where Jane's light footprints go.

No hound peals thus in wicked joy,
He snaps his muzzle in the snows,
        His five-clawed feet
        Now scamper fleet

Where Jane's bright lanthorn shows,
    Where Jane's bright lanthorn shows.

His hungry face stares out unseen
On hers as pure as wilding rose,
      Her amber eyes
      In fear's surprise
Watch largely as she goes,
    Watch largely as she goes.

Salt wells his hunger in his jaws,
His lust it revels to and fro
      Yet small beneath
      A soft voice saith,
" Jane shall in safety go,
    Jane shall in safety go."

He lurched as if a fiery lash
Had scourged his hide, and through, and through
      His furious eyes
      O'erscanned the skies,
But nearer dared not go,
    But nearer dared not go.

He reared like wild Bucephalus,
His fangs like spears in him uprose,
      Ev'n to the town
      Jane's flitting gown
He grins on as she goes,
    He grins on as she goes.

In fierce lament he howls amain,
He scampers, marvelling in this throes
      What brought him there
      To sup on air,
While Jane unharmèd goes,
    While Jane unharmèd goes.

CAKE AND SACK

Old King Caraway
    Supped on cake,
And a cup of sack
    His thirst to slake;
Bird in arras
    And hound in hall
Watched very softly
    Or not at all;
Fire in the middle,
    Stone all round

Changed not, heeded not,
    Made no sound;
All by himself
    At the Table High
He'd nibble and sip
    While his dreams slipped by;
And when he had finished,
    He'd nod and say,
" Cake and sack
    For King Caraway! "

NOW ALL THE ROADS

Now all the roads to London Town
Are windy-white with snow;
There's shouting and cursing,
And snortings to and fro;
But when night hangs her hundred lamps,
And the snickering frost-fires creep,
Then still, O; dale and hill, O;
Snow's fall'n deep.
Then still, O; dale and hill, O;
Snow's fall'n deep.

The carter cracks his leathery whip;
The ostler shouts Gee-whoa;
The farm dog grunts and sniffs and snuffs;
Bleat sheep; and cattle blow;
Soon Moll and Nan in dream are laid,
And snoring Dick's asleep;
Then still, O; dale and hill, O;
Snow's fall'n deep.
Then still, O; dale and hill, O;
Snow's fall'n deep.

[184]

THE SNOWFLAKE

Before I melt,
Come, look at me!
This lovely icy filigree!
Of a great forest
In one night
I make a wilderness
Of white:

By skyey cold
Of crystals made,
All softly, on
Your finger laid,
I pause, that you
My beauty see:
Breathe, and I vanish
Instantly.

THE FAIRY IN WINTER

There was a Fairy — flake of winter —
Who, when the snow came, whispering, Silence,
Sister crystal to crystal sighing,
Making of meadow argent palace,
    Night a star-sown solitude,
Cried 'neath her frozen eaves, " I burn here! "

Wings diaphanous, beating bee-like,
Wand within fingers, locks enspangled,
Icicle foot, lip sharp as scarlet,
She lifted her eyes in her pitch-black hollow —
Green as stalks of weeds in water —
Breathed: stirred.

Rilled from her heart the ichor, coursing,
Flamed and awoke her slumbering magic.
Softlier than moth's her pinions trembled;
Out into blackness, light-like, she flittered,
Leaving her hollow cold, forsaken.

In air, o'er crystal, rang twangling night-wind.
Bare, rimed pine-woods murmured lament.

[185]

ICE

The North Wind sighed:
And in a trice
What was water
Now is ice.

What sweet rippling
Water was
Now bewitched is
Into glass:

White and brittle
Where is seen
The prisoned milfoil's
Tender green;

Clear and ringing,
With sun aglow,
Where the boys sliding
And skating go.

Now furred 's each stick
And stalk and blade
With crystals out of
Dewdrops made.

Worms and ants
Flies, snails and bees
Keep close house-guard,
Lest they freeze;

Oh, with how sad
And solemn an eye
Each fish stares up
Into the sky.

In dread lest his
Wide watery home
At night shall solid
Ice become.

NOWEL

Holly dark: pale Mistletoe —
Christmas Eve is come, and lo,
Wild clash the bells across the snow,
Waits in the dark streets carolling go;
" Nowel! Nowel! " they shout — and, oh,
    How live out the day!
Each breath I breathe turns to a sigh;
    My heart is flown away;
The things I see around me seem
Entranced with light — as in a dream;
The candles dazzle in my eyes,
And every leaping fireflame tries
    To sing, what none could say.

THE QUARTETTE

Tom sang for joy and Ned sang for joy and old Sam sang for joy;
All we four boys piped up loud, just like one boy;
And the ladies that sate with the Squire — their cheeks were all wet,
For the noise of the voice of us boys, when we sang our Quartette.

Tom he piped low and Ned he piped low and Sam he piped low;
Into a sorrowful fall did our music flow;
And the ladies that sate with the Squire vowed they'd never forget,
How the eyes of them cried for delight, when we sang our Quartette.

SANTA CLAUS

" Hast thou, in Fancy, trodden where lie
Leagues of ice beneath the sky?
Where bergs, like palaces of light,
Emerald, sapphire, crystal white,
Glimmer in the polar night?

[187]

Hast thou heard in dead of dark
The mighty Sea-lion's shuddering bark?
Seen, shuffling through the crusted snow,
The blue-eyed Bears a-hunting go?
And in leagues of space o'erhead —
Radiant Aurora's glory spread?
Hast thou? " " Why? " " My child, because
There dwells thy loved Santa Claus."

THE SECRET

Open your eyes! . . . Now, look, and see!
Those starry tapers in the tree
Keep a promise 'twixt you and me:
Every toy and trinket there
In our secret has a share:
The Fairy on the topmost spray
Hears every single word I say:
I love — and *love* you: and I would
Give you my life, too, if I could.

THE FEAST

Crackers, meringues, and pink blomonge —
 Eat not for eating's sake!
But where mincepies and turkey went,
 A corner keep for cake.
See, dear Mamma's best silver too —
 And all for Christmas' sake!

While we sit snug within; without,
 The frost bites bitter sharp.
Bleak is the tune cold Winter sings,
 As shrilly rings his harp.
And dawn will whiten on a waste.
Of wintry hills, and woods at rest,
Where stript of fruit are rose and thorn,

And famished birds flit mute, forlorn.
No, not a morsel good to taste,
Nor drop to drink — unless there come
Some friendly human, with fingers numb,
To bring them dainties — such as these:
Crusts, hemp-seed, marrow-bones and cheese.

THE PANTOMIME

Were those fine horses once white Mice,
    Their Coachman an old Rat,
And the coach itself of the shape of a melon,
    There'd be good reason that
My pen should now attempt to tell a
    Tale entitled " Cinderella."

We see, it's true, a gentle face,
    As on the haughty henchmen pace;
But nowhere any hint, alas,
    Her two small slippers are made of glass.

It may be then the Stage is set
For quite a different Play; that this
Vast Castle, with its moated walls,
    The wild Aladdin's is —
Which, in the Scene that follows, may
Be magicked off to Africa.
Or Puss in Boots? Or Bluebeard's fell?
Or valiant Mollie Whuppie's? Well,
    We guess, but cannot tell.

Or are these pennons, this wild array
To welcome one who rode away,
Pillion upon a dapple-grey,
In the flush of the morning, in month of May?
    We ask, but cannot say.

MISTLETOE

Sitting under the mistletoe
(Pale-green, fairy mistletoe),
One last candle burning low,
All the sleepy dancers gone,
Just one candle burning on,
Shadows lurking everywhere:
Some one came, and kissed me there.

Tired I was; my head would go
Nodding under the mistletoe
(Pale-green, fairy mistletoe);
No footsteps came, no voice, but only,
Just as I sat there, sleepy, lonely,
Stooped in the still and shadowy air
Lips unseen — and kissed me there.

WINTER

Green Mistletoe!
Oh, I remember now
A dell of snow,
Frost on the bough;
None there but I:
Snow, snow; and a wintry sky.

None there but I,
And footprints one by one,
Zigzaggedly,
Where I had run;
Where shrill and powdery
A robin sat in the tree.

And he whistled sweet;
And I in the crusted snow
With snow-clubbed feet
Jigged to and fro,

Till, from the day,
The rose-light ebbed away.

And the robin flew
Into the air, the air,
The white mist through;
And small and rare
The night-frost fell
Into the calm and misty dell.

And the dusk gathered low,
And the silver moon and stars
On the frozen snow
Drew taper bars,
Kindled winking fires
In the hooded briers.

And the sprawling Bear
Growled deep in the sky;
And Orion's hair
Streamed sparkling by:
But the North sighed low,
" Snow, snow — more snow! "

Books
and
Stories

BLAISDELL

THE PICTURE-BOOK

Dear Reader, prythee, stay, and look
At this delightful Picture-Book!
Others like it you'll have seen,
For eye and mind to linger in,
But surely none, for tints and tones,
Lovelier than this — by Harold Jones?
Is there a colour —.earth, sky, sea,
Which from his box can missing be?
Even a Rainbow might whisper, Hush!
In envy of his paints and brush.

See with what heedful skill and grace
His patient pencil fills his space;
How stroke by stroke, and stage by stage,
He fits his pattern to the page,
And shows in every hue and line
Not only joy in his design,
But all that he takes such pleasure in.
Even his commonest objects tell
His love for what he sees so well.
And such is the delight he shows —
In stool or table, bird or rose —
That, sharing them, one hardly knows
Which for pleasure gives richer cause —
What he draws, or *how* he draws.

Things far and near so real are seen
You'd think the air flowed in between,
Yet touch of finger shows us that
The page itself is paper-flat!
Look once: again: and yet again —
Some fresh delight will still remain.
And though (I should confess betimes),
There was no need at all for rhymes,
'Twas yet the more a joy to tell,
If only in headlong doggerel,
What rich and lively company
This Picture-Book has been to me.

LISTEN!

Quiet your faces; be crossed every thumb;
Fix on me deep your eyes;
And out of my mind a story shall come,
Old, and lovely, and wise.

Old as the pebbles that fringe the cold seas,
Lovely as apples in rain;
Wise as the King who learned of the bees,
Then learned of the emmets again.

Old as the fruits that in mistletoe shine;
Lovely as amber, as snow;
Wise as the fool who when care made to pine
Cried, Hey and fol lol, lilly lo!

Old as the woods rhyming Thomas snuffed sweet,
When pillion he rode with the Queen:
Lovely as elf-craft; wise as the street
Where the roofs of the humble are seen. . . .

Ay, there's a stirring, there's wind in the bough;
Hearken, a harp I hear ring:
Like a river of water my story shall flow
Like linnets of silver sing.

" SUPPOSE "

" Suppose . . . and suppose that a wild little Horse of Magic
Came cantering out of the sky,
With bridle of silver, and into the saddle I mounted,
To fly — and to fly;

" And we stretched up into the air, fleeting on in the sunshine,
A speck in the gleam
On galloping hoofs, his mane in the wind out-flowing,
In a shadowy stream;

[196]

" And, oh, when at last the gentle star of evening
Came crinkling into the blue,
A magical castle we saw in the air, like a cloud of moonlight,
As onward we flew;

" And across the green moat on the drawbridge we foamed and we
    snorted,
And there was a beautiful Queen
Who smiled at me strangely; and spoke to my wild little horse,
    too —
A lovely and beautiful Queen;

" And she cried with delight — and delight — to her delicate
    maidens,
Behold my daughter — my dear!

And they crowned me with flowers, and then to their harps sate
    playing,
Solemn and clear;

" And magical cakes and goblets were spread on the table;
And at window the birds came in;
Hopping along with bright eyes, pecking crumbs from the platters,
And sipped of the wine;

" And splashing up — up to the roof tossed fountains of crystal;
And Princes in scarlet and green
Shot with their bows and arrows, and kneeled with their dishes
Of fruits for the Queen;

" And we walked in a magical garden with rivers and bowers,
And my bed was of ivory and gold;
And the Queen breathed soft in my ear a song of enchantment —
And I never grew old . . .

" And I never, never came back to the earth, oh, never and
    never . . .
How mother would cry and cry!
There'd be snow on the fields then, and all these sweet flowers in the
    winter
Would wither and die . . .

" Suppose . . . and suppose . . ."

THE MILLER AND HIS SON

A twangling harp for Mary,
    A silvery flute for John,
And now we'll play the livelong day,
    " The Miller and his Son.". . .

" The Miller went a-walking
    All in the forest high,
He sees three doves a-flitting
    Against the dark blue sky:

" Says he, ' My son, now follow
    These doves so white and free,
That cry above the forest,
    And surely cry to thee.'

" ' I go, my dearest Father,
    But Oh! I sadly fear,
These doves so white will lead me far,
    But never bring me near.'

" He kisses the Miller,
    He cries, ' Awhoop to ye! '
And straightway through the forest
    Follows the wood-doves three.

" There came a sound of weeping
    To the Miller in his Mill;
Red roses in a thicket
    Bloomed over near his wheel;

" Three stars shone wild and brightly
    Above the forest dim:
But never his dearest son
    Returns again to him.

"The cuckoo shall call 'Cuckoo!'
     In vain along the vale,
The linnet, and the blackbird,
     The mournful nightingale;

"The Miller hears and sees not,
     He's thinking of his son;
His toppling wheel is silent;
     His grinding done.

"'O doves so white!' he weepeth,
     'O roses on the tree!
O stars that shine so brightly —
     You shine in vain for me!'

"I bade him 'Follow, follow';
     He said, 'O Father dear,
These doves so white will lead me far
     But never bring me near!'"...

A twangling harp for Mary,
     A silvery flute for John,
And now we'll play the livelong day,
     "The Miller and his Son."

THE CHILD IN THE STORY GOES TO BED

I prythee, Nurse, come smooth my hair,
     And prythee, Nurse, unloose my shoe,
And trimly turn my silken sheet
     Upon my quilt of gentle blue.

My pillow sweet of lavender
     Smooth with an amiable hand,
And may the dark pass peacefully by
     As in the hour-glass droops the sand.

Prepare my cornered manchet sweet,
　　And in my little crystal cup
Pour out the blithe and flowering mead
　　That forthwith I may sup.

Withdraw my curtains from the night,
　　And let the crispèd crescent shine
Upon my eyelids while I sleep,
　　And soothe me with her beams benign.

Dark looms the forest far-away;
　　O, listen! through its empty dales
Rings from the solemn echoing boughs
　　The music of its nightingales.

Now quench my silver lamp, prythee,
　　And bid the harpers harp that tune
Fairies that haunt the meadowlands
　　Sing to the stars of June.

And bid them play, though I in dreams
　　No longer heed their pining strains,
For I would not to silence wake
　　When slumber o'er my senses wanes.

You Angels bright who me defend,
　　Enshadow me with curvèd wing,
And keep me in the long dark night
　　Till dawn another day shall bring.

THE CHILD IN THE STORY AWAKES

The light of dawn rose on my dreams,
　　And from afar I seemed to hear
In sleep the mellow blackbird call
　　Hollow and sweet and clear.

I prythee, Nurse, my casement open,
    Wildly the garden peals with singing,
And hooting through the dewy pines
    The goblins of the dark are winging.

O listen the droning of the bees,
    That in the roses take delight!
And see a cloud stays in the blue
    Like an angel still and bright.

The gentle sky is spread like silk,
    And, Nurse, the moon doth languish there,
As if it were a perfect jewel
    In the morning's soft-spun hair.

The greyness of the distant hills
    Is silvered in the lucid East,
See, now the sheeny-plumèd cock
    Wags haughtily his crest.

" O come you out, O come you out,
    Lily, and lavender, and lime;
The kingcup swings his golden bell,
    And plumpy cherries drum the time.

" O come you out, O come you out!
    Roses, and dew, and mignonette,
The sun is in the steep blue sky,
    Sweetly the morning star is set."

THE SLEEPING BEAUTY

The scent of bramble fills the air,
    Amid her folded sheets she lies,
The gold of evening in her hair,
    The blue of morn shut in her eyes.

[202]

How many a changing moon hath lit
    The unchanging roses of her face!
Her mirror ever broods on it
    In silver stillness of the days.

Oft flits the the moth on filmy wings
    Into his solitary lair;
Shrill evensong the cricket sings
    From some still shadow in her hair.

In heat, in snow, in wind, in flood,
    She sleeps in lovely loneliness,
Half-folded like an April bud
    On winter-haunted trees.

REVERIE

When slim Sophia mounts her horse
    And paces down the avenue,
It seems an inward melody
    She paces to.

Each narrow hoof is lifted high
    Beneath the dark enclustering pines,
A silver ray within his bit
    And bridle shines.

His eye burns deep, his tail is arched,
    And streams upon the shadowy air,
The daylight sleeks his jetty flanks,
    His mistress' hair.

Her habit flows in darkness down,
    Upon the stirrup rests her foot,
Her brow is lifted, as if earth
    She heeded not.

'Tis silent in the avenue,
    The sombre pines are mute of song,
The blue is dark, there moves no breeze
    The boughs among.

When slim Sophia mounts her horse
    And paces down the avenue,
It seems an inward melody
    She paces to.

KING DAVID

King David was a sorrowful man:
    No cause for his sorrow had he:
And he called for the music of a hundred harps,
    To solace his melancholy.

They played till they all fell silent:
    Played — and play sweet did they;
But the sorrow that haunted the heart of King David
    They could not charm away.

He rose; and in his garden
    Walked by the moon alone,
A nightingale hidden in a cypress-tree
    Jargoned on and on.

King David lifted his sad eyes
    Into the dark-boughed tree —
" Tell me, thou little bird that singest,
    Who taught my grief to thee? "

But the bird in no wise heeded;
    And the king in the cool of the moon
Hearkened to the nightingale's sorrowfulness,
    Till all his own was gone.

THEN AS NOW

Then as Now; and Now as Then,
Spins on this World of Men.
White — Black — Yellow — Red:
They wake, work, eat, play, go to bed.
Black — Yellow — Red — White:
They talk, laugh, weep, dance, morn to night.
Yellow — Red — White — Black:
Sun shines, moon rides, clouds come back.
Red — White — Black — Yellow:
Count your hardest, who could tell o'
The myriads that have come and gone,
Stayed their stay this earth upon,
And vanished then, their labour done?
Sands of the wilderness, stars in heaven,
Solomon could not sum them even:
Then as Now; Now as Then
Still spins on this World of Men.

KINGS AND QUEENS

Eight Henries, one Mary,
    One Elizabeth;
Crowned and throned Kings and Queens
    Now lie still in death.

Four Williams, one Stephen,
    Anne, Victoria, John:
Sceptre and orb are laid aside;
    All are to quiet gone.
And James and Charles, and Charles's sons —
    They, too, have journeyed on.

Three Richards, seven Edwards
    Their royal hour did thrive;
They sleep with Georges one to four:
    And we praise God for five.

THE OLD KING

Woke — the old King of Cumberland:
    Yet breathed not nor stirred,
But crouched in the darkness, hearkening after
    A voice he had heard.

He leaned upon his foursquare bed,
    Thumb beneath bristling chin;
" Alas, alas! — the woeful dream —
    The dream that I was in! "

The old, old King of Cumberland
    Muttered, " Twas not the sea
Gushing upon Schlievlisskin rocks
    That wakened me.

" Thunder from midmost night it was not,
    For yonder at those bars
Burn fiercely toward the Eastern deeps
    The summer stars."

The old, old King of Cumberland
    Mused yet, " Rats ever did
Ramp, rustle, clink my spurs, and gnaw
    My coverlid.

" Oft hath a furtive midnight breeze
    Along this valance skirred;
But in this stagnant calm 'twas not
    The wind I heard.

" Some keener, stranger, quieter, closer
    Voice it was me woke . . ."
And silence, like a billow, drowned
    The word he spoke.

Fixed now his stare, for limned in dark,
    Gazing from cowl-like hood,
Stark in the vague, all-listening night,
    A shadow stood.

Sudden a gigantic hand he thrust
    Into his bosom cold,
Where now no surging restless beat
    Its long tale told.

Swept on him then, as there he sate,
    Terror icy chill:
'Twas silence that had him awoke —
    His heart stood still.

THE CORNER

Good News to tell!
Oh, mark it well!
Old Mr. Jones,
Once all but bones —
There never was
A sight forlorner —
At last, at last,
All danger past,
Has been and gone and
Turned the corner;
And every hour
Is growing younger.

A week ago,
By Almanac,
His long white beard
Went jetty black,
The red into his cheeks
Came back.

His teeth were sharp
And thirty-two,
His faded eyes
A bright bird-blue.
When two-three days
Were scarcely run,
He slips from forty
To twenty-one;
He skips and dances,
Heel and toe;
He couldn't downwards
Quicker grow.
All that he'd learned
Began to go;
His memory melted
Just like snow.

At plump four foot
He burst his stitches,

His trousers dwindled
Back to breeches;
The breeches gone,
There came short clothes,
Two dumpling cheeks,
A button nose,
A mop of curls,
Ten crinkled toes.
And now as fast
As he is able,
He's nestling down
Into his cradle.

Old Mrs. Jones,
With piping eye,
She rocks, and croons
Him *Hushaby*.
Last Sunday gone,
He turned the corner,
And still grows
Younger, younger, younger . . .
Old Mr. Jones.

TILLIE

Old Tillie Turveycombe
Sat to sew,
Just where a patch of fern did
    grow;
There, as she yawned,
And yawn wide did she,
Floated some seed
Down her gull-e-t;
And look you once,
And look you twice,

Poor old Tillie
Was gone in a trice.
But oh, when the wind
Do a-moaning come,
'Tis poor old Tillie
Sick for home;
And oh, when a voice
In the mist do sigh,
Old Tillie Turveycombe's
Floating by.

SAM'S THREE WISHES:
or LIFE'S LITTLE WHIRLIGIG

"I'm thinking and thinking," said old Sam Shore,
'Twere somebody *knocking* I heard at the door."

From the clock popped the cuckoo and cuckooed out eight,
As there in his chair he wondering sate . . .

[208]

" There's no-one I knows on would come so late,
A-clicking the latch of an empty house
With nobbut inside 'un but me and a mouse. . . .
Maybe a-waking in sleep I be,
And 'twere out of a dream came that tapping to me."
At length he cautiously rose, and went,
And with thumb upon latch awhile listening bent,
Then slowly drew open the door. And behold!
There stood a Fairy — all green and gold,
Mantled up warm against dark and cold,
And smiling up into his candleshine,
Lips like wax, and cheeks like wine,
As saucy and winsome a thing to see
As are linden buds on a linden tree.

Stock-still in the doorway stood simple Sam,
A-ducking his head, with " Good-e'en to 'ee, Ma'am."

Dame Fairy she nods, and cries clear and sweet,
" 'Tis a *very* good-e'en, sir, when such folks meet.
I know thee, Sam, though thou wist not of me,
And I come in late gloaming to speak with thee;
Though my eyes do dazzle at glint of your rush,
All under this pretty green fuchsia bush."

Sam ducked once more, smiling simple and slow.
Like the warbling of birds her words did flow,
And she laughed, very merry, to see how true
Shone the old man's kindness his courtesy through.
And she nodded her head, and the stars on high
Sparkled down on her smallness from out of the sky.

" A friend is a friend, Sam, and wonderful pleasant,
And I'm come for old sake's sake to bring thee a present.
Three wishes, three wishes are thine, Sam Shore,
Just three wishes — and wish no more.
All for because, ruby-ripe to see,
The pixy-pears burn in yon hawthorn tree,
And the old milch cow, wheresoever she goes,

Never crops over the fairy-knowes.
Ay, Sam, thou art old and thy house is lone,
But there's Potencies round thee, and here is one!"

Poor Sam, he stared: and the stars o'erhead
A shimmering light on the elm-tops shed.
Like rilling of water her voice rang sweet,
And the night-wind sighed at the sound of it.
He frowned — glanced back at the empty grate,
And shook very slowly his grey old pate:
"Three wishes, my dear! Why, I scarcely knows
Which be my crany and which my toes.
But I thank 'ee, Ma'am, kindly, and this I'd say,
That the night of your passing is Michaelmas Day;
And if it were company come on a sudden,
Why, I'd ax for a fat goose to fry in the oven!"

And lo, and forsooth! as the words he was uttering,
A rich puff of air set his candle a-guttering,
And there rose in the kitchen a sizzling and sputtering,
With a crackling of sparks and of flames a great fluttering,
And — of which there could not be two opinions —
A smoking-hot savour of sage and onions.
Beam, wall and flagstones the kitchen was lit,
Every dark corner and cranny of it,
With the blaze from the hearthstone. Copper and brass
Winked back the winking of platter and glass.
And a wonderful squeaking of mice went up
At the smell of a Michaelmas supper to sup —
Unctuous odours that wreathed and swirled
Where'er frisked a whisker or mouse-tail twirled,
While out of the chimney up into the night
That ne'er-to-be-snuffed-too-much smoke took flight.

"That's one," says the Fairy, finger on thumb,
"So now, Mister Sam, there's but two to come!"
She leaned her head sidelong; she lifted her chin,
With a twinkling of eye from the radiance within.
Poor Sam stood stounded; he says, says he,

" I *wish* my old Mother was back with me,
For if there was one thing she couldn't refuse
'Twas a sweet thick slice from the breast of a goose."
But his cheek grew stiff, and his eyes stared bright,
For there, on her stick, pushing out of the night,
Tap-tapping along, herself and no other,
Came who but the shape of his dear old Mother!
Straight into the kitchen she hastened and went,
Her breath coming quick as if all but spent,
" Why, Sam," says she, " the bird be turning,
For my nose tells I that the skin's a-burning! "
And down at the oven the ghost of her sat,
And basted the goose with the boiling fat.

" Oho," cries the Fairy, sweet and small,
" Another wish gone will leave nothing at all."
And Sam sighs, " Bless 'ee, Ma'am, keep the other,
There's nowt that I want now I have my Mother."
But the Fairy laughs softly, and says, says she,
" There's one wish left, Sam, I promised 'ee three.
Hasten thy wits, the hour creeps on,
There's calling afield, and I'm soon to be gone.
Soon as haps midnight the cocks will crow,
And me to the gathering and feasting must go."

Sam gazed at his Mother — withered and wan,
The rose in her cheek, her bright hair, gone,
And her poor old back bent double with years —
And he scarce could speak for the salt, salt tears.
" Well, well," he says, " I'm unspeakable glad;
But — it bain't quite the same as when I was a lad.
There's joy and there's joy, Ma'am, but to tell 'ee the truth
There's none can compare with the joy of one's youth.
And if it was possible, how could I choose
But be back in boy's breeches to eat the goose;
And all the old things — and my Mother the most,
To shine again real as my own gatepost.
What wouldn't I give, too, to see again wag

The dumpity tail of my old dog, Shag!
Your kindness, Ma'am: but all wishing was vain
Unless us can both be young again."

A shrill, faint laughter from nowhere came . . .
Empty the dark in the candle-flame. . . .

And there stood our Sam, about four foot high,
Snub nose, shock hair, and round blue eye.
Breeches and braces, and coat of him too,
Shirt on his back, and each clodhopping shoe
Had shrunk to a nicety — button and hem
To fit the small Sammie tucked up into them.
There was his Mother, too; smooth, clear cheek,
Lips as smooth as a blackbird's beak,
Pretty arched eyebrows, the daintiest nose —
While the smoke of the baking deliciously rose.

" Come, Sammie," she cries, " your old Mammikin's joy,
Climb up on your stool, supper's ready, my boy.
Bring in the candle, and shut out the night;
There's goose, baked taties and cabbage to bite.
Why, bless the wee lamb, he's all shiver and shake,
And you'd think from the look of him scarcely awake!
If 'ee glour wi' those eyes, Sam, so dark and round,
The elves will away with 'ee, I'll be bound! "

So Sam and his mother by wishes three
Were made just as happy as happy can be.
And there — with a bumpity tail to wag —
Sat laughing, with tongue out, their old dog, Shag.
To clatter of platter, bones, giblets, and juice,
Between them they ate up the whole of the goose.

But time is a river for ever in flow,
The weeks went by as the weeks must go.
Soon fifty-two to a year did grow.
The long years passed, one after another,
Making older and older our Sam and his mother;

And, alas and alack, with nine of them gone,
Poor Shag lay asleep again under a stone.
And a sorrowful dread would sometimes creep
Into Sam's dreams, as he lay asleep,
That his Mother was lost, and away he'd fare,
Calling her, calling her, everywhere,
In dark, in rain, by roads unknown,
Under echoing hills, and alone, alone.
What bliss in the morning to wake and see
The sun shining green in the linden tree,
And out of that dream's dark shadowiness
To slip in on his Mother and give her a kiss,
Then go whistling off in the dew to hear
The thrushes all mocking him, sweet and clear.

Still, moon after moon from heaven above
Shone on Mother and son, and made light of love.
Her roses faded, her pretty brown hair
Had sorrowful grey in it everywhere.
And at last she died, and was laid to rest,
Her tired hands crossed on her shrunken breast.
And Sam, now lonely, lived on and on
Till most of his workaday life seemed gone.

Yet spring came again with its green and blue,
And presently summer's wild roses too,
Pinks, Sweet William, and sops-in-wine,
Blackberry, lavender, eglantine.
And when these had blossomed and gone their way,
'Twas apples, and daisies and Michaelmas Day —
Yes, spider-webs, dew, and haws in the may,
And seraphs singing in Michaelmas Day.

Sam worked all morning and *couldn't* get rest
For a kind of a feeling of grief in his breast.
And yet, not grief, but something more
Like the thought that what happens has happened before.
He fed the chickens, he fed the sow,
On a three-legged stool sate down to the cow,

[213]

With a pail 'twixt his legs in the green of the meadow,
Under the elm trees' lengthening shadow;
And woke at last with a smile and a sigh
To find he had milked his poor Jingo dry.

As dusk set in, the birds did seem
To be calling and whistling from out of a dream.
He chopped up kindling, shut up his shed,
In a bucket of well-water soused his head
To freshen his eyes up a little and make
The drowsy old wits of him wider awake.
As neat as a womanless creature is able
He swept up his hearthstone, and laid the table.
And then o'er his platter and mug, if you please,
Sate gloomily gooming at loaf and cheese —
Gooming and gooming as if the mere sight
Of his victuals could satisfy appetite!
And the longer and longer he looked at them,
The slimmer slimmed upward his candle-flame,
Blue in the air. And when squeaked a mouse
'Twas loud as a trump in the hush of the house.
Then, sudden, a soft little wind puffed by,
'Twixt the thick-thatched roof and the star-sown sky;
And died . . . And then
That deep, dead, wonderful silence again.

Then — soft as a rattle counting her seeds
In the midst of a tangle of withered-up weeds —
Came a faint, faint knocking, a rustle like silk,
And a breath at the keyhole as soft as milk —
Still as the flit of a moth. And then . . .
That infinitesimal knocking again.
Sam lifted his chin from his fists. He listened.
His wandering eyes in the candle glistened.
Then slowly, slowly, rolled round by degrees —
And there sat a mouse on the top of his cheese.
He stared at this Midget, and it at him,
Over the edge of his mug's round rim,

[214]

And — as if it were Christian — he says, " Did 'ee hear
A faint little tap-tap-tap-tapping, my dear?
You was at supper, and me in a maze,
'Tis dark for a caller in these lone days,
There's nowt in the larder. We're both of us old,
And all of my loved ones sleep under the mould,
And yet — and yet — as I've told 'ee before . . .

But if Sam's story you'd read to the end,
Turn back to page 1, and press onward, dear friend;
Yes, if you would stave the last note of this song,
Turn back to page primus, and warble along!
For all sober records of life (come to write 'em),
Are bound to continue — well — ad infinitum!

PIGS

A cock it was, in the stable yard,
That reared its crest with shimmering plume,
And crowed till all the fields around
    Re-echoed in the gloom.

Up got the landlord, and looked out —
" What ails the bird! So shrill he cries! "
How should he dream this farmyard prince
    Was more than earthly wise?

How should he dream that over the bridge
That spans the lilies of Ullone
The Witch of the Woods now winsome rides
    Her milk-white ass upon?

And down she comes with nodding flowers
Into the Inn's cool quietness;
" Heh, bring me butter and honeycomb,
    And I this house will bless! "

[215]

She breaks with finger and with thumb
The waxen honeycomb; she quaffs
Of the sweet buttermilk; and turns —
    Turns to the house and laughs:

" Mimsey and mo, I thirsty was! "
Then looks she on the garden fruits,
Which hung upon the branches green
    Bowed almost to the roots.

" Prythee," she says, " my pigs let come
Into your orchard when the moon
Eyes with a red and fiery face
    The harvest of Ullone."

Says he, " Small custom comes this way.
Can man make cider out of mast!
With all my apples fattening pigs,
    What's left for me at last?

" With all my codlins crunched for ham — "
His rage broke out, his green eyes shone —
" Thou muncher of poor man's honeycomb!
    Begone, thou Witch, begone! "

He frowned upon her waxen cheek,
Her sloe-black eyes, her smooth-drawn hair;
And she looked back, the woeful witch,
    Straddling her saddle there.

She lightly plucked her bridle rein,
She wheeled her milk-white ass aside,
And, stooped in her laughter, turned:
    But not one word replied. . . .

And soon it was the midnight hour;
And large the moon was mounted up
Into the night's dark hollow roof,
    When came her pigs to sup.

They pattered like hailstones over the bridge,
And, like the mandrake, squealed: and soon
In the deep orchard-grasses lay
    No fruit beneath the moon.

Then cried the landlord, peeping out —
" Oddslife! and I no payment take! " —
And out into the yard he stole,
    His burning ire to slake.

Sticks — sticks he in his knife, plumb-deep. . . .
When, suddenly, like a story told,
Age, like a withered mantle, falls,
    And all things doth enfold.

He sees his Inn a ruin hoar,
Mantled with ivy thick and close,
Wherein a host of fearless birds
    In tumult comes and goes.

He sees his gnarled grey apple trees
Bent like old men, and fruitless all;
He sees a broken bridge lead down
    To a wild waterfall.

And on the hand that holds his knife
Age hath turned white the scattered hairs;
And in his ear a wind makes moan
    In drear and dreamy airs. . . .

Still stoops that green and mantled Inn;
Still o'er the mixen, lank doth range
Old Chanticleer with wattles wan,
    And whoop unearthly strange.

The old fox skulks, more grey than red,
Between the lichen-cankered boles;
And all about the blackened thatch
    The starlings make their holes.

And from a window dense in leaves
And smitten with the first moonbeam,
An owl-face peers, whose real is now
    The sorcery of a dream.

And still, when autumn spiders spin,
And Michael's daisy spreads its mauve,
Out from the gloom of dark Ullone
    Ramp piglings, drove on drove.

Then dwindles one lone ghostly crow;
Hesper a silver arrow flings;
And faint from out of the far-away,
    A snow-white blackbird sings.

THE THIEF AT ROBIN'S CASTLE

There came a Thief one night to Robin's Castle,
    He climbed up into a Tree;
And sitting with his head among the branches,
    A wondrous Sight did see.

For there was Robin supping at his table,
    With Candles of pure Wax,
His Dame and his two beauteous little Children,
    With Velvet on their backs.

Platters for each there were shin-shining,
    Of Silver many a pound,
And all of beaten Gold, three brimming Goblets,
    Standing the table round.

The smell that rose up richly from the Baked Meats
    Came thinning amid the boughs,
And much that greedy Thief who snuffed the night air —
    His Hunger did arouse.

He watched them eating, drinking, laughing, talking,
    Busy with finger and spoon,
While three most cunning Fiddlers, clad in crimson,
    Played them a supper-tune.

And he waited in the tree-top like a Starling,
    Till the Moon was gotten low;
When all the windows in the walls were darkened,
    He softly in did go.

There Robin and his Dame in bed were sleeping,
    And his Children young and fair;
Only Robin's Hounds from their warm kennels
    Yelped as he climbed the stair.

All, all were sleeping, page and fiddler,
    Cook, scullion, free from care;
Only Robin's Stallions from their stables
    Neighed as he climbed the stair.

A wee wan light the Moon did shed him,
    Hanging above the sea,
And he counted into his bag (of beaten Silver)
    Platters thirty-three.

Of Spoons three score; of jolly golden Goblets
    He stowed in four save one,
And six fine three-branched Cupid Candlesticks,
    Before his work was done.

Nine bulging bags of Money in a cupboard,
    Two Snuffers and a Dish
He found, the last all studded with great Garnets
    And shapen like a Fish.

Then tiptoe up he stole into a Chamber,
    Where on Tasselled Pillows lay
Robin and his Dame in dreaming slumber,
    Tired with the summer's day.

That Thief he mimbled round him in the gloaming,
    Their Treasures for to spy,
Combs, Brooches, Chains, and Rings, and Pins and Buckles
    All higgledy piggle-dy.

A Watch shaped in the shape of a flat Apple
    In purest Crystal set,
He lifted from the hook where it was ticking
    And crammed in his Pochette.

He heaped the pretty Baubles on the table,
    Trinkets, Knick-knackerie,
Pearls, Diamonds, Sapphires, Topazes, and Opals —
    All in his bag put he.

And there in night's pale Gloom was Robin dreaming
    He was hunting the mountain Bear,
While his Dame in peaceful slumber in no wise heeded
    A greedy Thief was there.

And that ravenous Thief he climbed up even higher,
    Till into a chamber small
He crept where lay poor Robin's beauteous Children,
    Lovelier in sleep withal.

Oh, fairer was their Hair than Gold of Goblet,
    'Yond Silver their Cheeks did shine,
And their little hands that lay upon the linen
    Made that Thief's hard heart to pine.

But though a moment there his hard heart faltered,
    Eftsoones he took the twain,
Slipped them into his Bag with all his Plunder,
    And softly stole down again.

Spoon, Platter, Goblet, Ducats, Dishes, Trinkets,
    And those two Children dear,
A-quaking in the clinking and the clanking,
    And half bemused with fear,

He carried down the stairs into the Courtyard,
  But there he made no stay,
He just tied up his Garters, took a deep breath,
  And ran like the wind away.

Past Forest, River, Mountain, River, Forest —
  He coursed the whole night through,
Till morning found him come into a Country,
  Where none his bad face knew.

Past Mountain, River, Forest, River, Mountain —
  That Thief's lean shanks sped on,
Till Evening found him knocking at a Dark House,
  His breath now well-nigh gone.

There came a little maid and asked his Business;
  A Cobbler dwelt within;
And though she much disliked the Bag he carried,
  She led the Bad Man in.

He bargained with the Cobbler for a lodging
  And soft laid down his Sack —
In the Dead of Night, with none to spy or listen —
  From off his weary Back.

And he taught the little Chicks to call him Father,
  And he sold his stolen Pelf,
And bought a Palace, Horses, Slaves, and Peacocks,
  To ease his wicked self.

And though the Children never really loved him,
  He was rich past all belief;
While Robin and his Dame o'er Delf and Pewter
  Spent all their Days in Grief.

BOOKS

A boy called Jack, as I've been told,
Would sit for hours — good as gold —
Not with a pie, like Master Horner,
And plums, for dainties, in his corner,
But silent in some chosen nook,
And spell-bound — by a story-book!
Whether the dawn brought sun or rain,
Back to its pages he'd hasten again;
He had even wheedled from his friends
A secret hoard of candle-ends,
And — slumber far from his round head —
Would read, till dead of night — in bed!

How often his mother would sigh, and cry —
" Up, Jack, and put that trumpery by!
    See, Spring is in the sky!
The swallow is here, the thorn's in blow —
Crimson, pink, and driven snow;
Lambs caper in the fields; and there,
Cuckoo flies calling through the air;
    Oh, why stay in? Oh, why? "

And Jack would smile. . . . No wonder! He
In books found marvellous company,
Wonder, romance, and mystery.
He pined to follow, on and on,
Sailors on strange adventure gone;
With travellers to rove, and scan
Regions untrodden by mortal man.
Eyes shining, breathless, cramped, stock-still,
Lost in these dreams he'd crouch until
The fancied all but seemed the real.
Tales old or new he read with zest,
But some he loved beyond the rest: —

That other Jack's, whose magic Beans
Led skyward to a Giant's demesnes —

His Money Bags, Harp — centuries old,
The Hen that laid him eggs of gold:

And starving Dick's who ran away,
But heard Bow Bells up Highgate Way,
Entreating him turn back again.
The which he did. And not in vain!
Since close behind him, sleek and spruce,
Came trotting on his faithful Puss.
'Twas she who rid the soot-black Chief
Of rats in myriads past belief,
Which, when he lay in deep repose,
Would nip his fingers, gnaw his toes;
And while at meat he sat, in State,
Would drag the beef bones off his plate!
A mort of money, in coffers fat,
This Moor paid down for such a Cat.
These shipped, Dick then sailed home at once,
With casks cram-full of precious stones;
And, having given her all he had brought her,
Won for his bride his master's daughter
(A lass as sweet as she was fair),
And thrice was London's loved Lord Mayor.

Gulliver, too; who, shipwrecked, woke,
Arms, legs pegged down by pygmy folk,
With needle arrows, bows of gut,
Who fifteen hundred horses brought,
And dragged him off to Lilliput.
When two explored his box of snuff
They nearly sneezed their cranies off.
Pitching a ladder against his side,
They rambled over him, far and wide —
As emmets on a pumpkin creep.
They fed him fat on tiny sheep;
Startled, like birds, at every wink,
Poured puncheons down his throat for drink.
Church-high he paced along their streets;
For handkerchiefs they gave him sheets;

And when they went to War, then he
Tugged their whole Navy out to sea.

He sailed once more, was wrecked again,
And seized by a Brobdingnagian,
Huge as an oak, his shoes to match,
And hair as thick as farmyard thatch,
Teeth like small milestones, eyes beside,
Like green glass marbles a cubit wide.
These towering bumpkins roared to see
A human imp minute as he;
Made him a mock, a toy — and worse,
Gave him a child to be his Nurse,
Fifty feet high. Her plaits of hair
Swung like gold hawsers in the air,
Her ribbons fluttered wide and far
Like pennons on a ship of war.
She loved him dearly — gentle soul,
Far more than even her favourite doll;
And made two boxes for the waif,
To carry him and keep him safe.
The woes he faced! — the horrid Ape
Which dandled him upon its lap,
Then snatched him up and scuttled off
To sport with him upon a roof
Whose rain-pipes when in overflow
Poured down five hundred feet below.
Perils beset him everywhere;
'Twas death to topple off a chair.
In nick of time he pinked a rat
Ferocious as a tiger-cat;
And, like Duke Clarence, drowned did seem
When rescued from a bowl of cream.
But courage will on danger thrive;
Not only cowards come home alive!

And Sindbad — tranced on Indian deep,
When shades of night began to creep —
Who took for land a Whale, asleep!

And, pushing off in a small boat,
To where this Monster lay afloat,
With his three shipmates, scrambled up
Its steep and slippery side — to sup.
There, having heaped the sun-dried wrack,
They lit a bonfire on its back.
A whisper through the Creature ran —
" Beware! Arouse thee! Danger! Man! "
It stirred; it woke; its drowsy eye
Fixed on the flame-flushed company —
Turban, sash, and matted hair —
Feasting, singing, carousing there.
There came a swirl of flukes and fin —
And then was nought where Whale had been!
Only a watery waste of sea
Where a strange Island had seemed to be!
And in its moonlight one black head —
Sindbad's, aghast with terror and dread,
His boon companions — drowned — and dead.
Ay, and 'twas Sindbad, too, who found —
When on a real isle marooned,
A Roc's egg — fifty paces round.
Teeth chattering, blanched with fear, he heard
The winged-beats of the mother bird,
Like distant thunder on the air;
And — darkening day — her shadow there,
In heaven. Down she swooped to rest,
A riot of splendour, on her nest.
Nearer, at length, he dared to draw,
And tied his body to her claw,
Scaled as with mail, its talons trim,
But broader than a weaver's beam.
She rose, soared high, and alighted in
A valley where a stream had been —
A gaunt and haunted wild abyss,
Scarped with a dizzying precipice.
And Sindbad stood, like one who is stunned,
At sight of a huge diamond —

Flashing its lightnings through the air.
Nay, thousands of blazing gems were there
In heaps — like apples in a pie.
And lo! aloft, against the sky,
Wheeled screaming eagles, starved for meat.
And merchants came . . .

        But every bit
Of these strange voyages Jack knew
All but by heart; and Crusoe's, too.
Bandage his eyes, I vow he would
Not falter in *his* Solitude! —
The wreck, the footprint, the stockade,
Cave, parrot, cats; the pots he made.
'Neath its great stars at will he'd rove
Hill and valley, creek and cove.
So close and often the tale he had read
He knew the Island as Friday did;
As if from home himself he'd run,
Worn Crusoe's goatskins, fired his gun.

Our Jack loved *all*. As dear to him
The tales of Andersen and Grimm.
He had roamed their pages through and through —
The Seven Swans; Rapunzel, too;
The Gnome whose secret was his name;
Hanzel and Gretel, who weeping came
To a cottage of cake and sweetmeats made,
Which, for a trap, a Witch had laid.
And Snow-White, whom the Dwarfs took in
To guard her from the wicked Queen.
She, envious of her lovely face,
Came, painted, to her hiding-place,
With poisoned comb, and bodice-lace.
"Taste, Sweet!" her wheedling tongue besought.
When she the fatal apple brought —
Pleasant to eye and sweet to lip.
One morsel; and in trance-like sleep —

A dreamless slumber, heavy as lead —
Poor Snow-White lay like one who is dead.
At evening from their copper mine
The merry Dwarfs came home to dine.
They found their Snow-White cold and still
As a wraith of flowers on an April hill.
Oh bitter grief! Alas! Alas!
They made her a coffin of crystal glass;
There to this day aswoon to lie,
Had not a Prince come riding by,
Who, marvelling at her loveliness,
Stooped low, and waked her — with a kiss.

Poetry, too, was Jack's delight;
He even rhymed in dreams at night;
Roving where every stream and tree
The haunt was of divinity;
Where lorn Esnalda, lost, astray,
In a wide forest, green with May,
Was found by an Elfin, and rode away
Pillion, upon a dapple-grey.
Knee-deep in flowers, sweet and wan,
He heard the enticing pipes of Pan;
And — where the waves in foam of snow
Shine in the gilding after-glow —
Hearkened, afar, that echoing
Shrill song the lovely sirens sing,
At eve in their rock-bound solitude.

Well, well — so Jack would sit and brood.
Book-crazed was he, and still read on;
His heart was where his eyes were gone.
Friends would come knocking might and main,
Make faces through the window-pane,
Call, whistle, taunt him — all in vain.
He hardly heeded what they said,
Lowered an inch or two his head,
And once more read — and read — and — read.

Ev'n finish a tale he would, and then
Devour it, every word, again!
All which is how, one might suppose,
A Jack into a *bookworm* grows —
A wretched thing, of paper made,
Timid, half-blind, caged-in, afraid;
And quite unable to enjoy
What pleases any other boy.

Never believe it! What Jack read
Refreshed his senses, heart, and head.
Words were to him not merely *words* —
Their sounds rang sweet as bells, or birds;
Nor could he tell, by any test,
Whether he loved — he once confessed —
Their music, or their meaning, best.
And all they pictured clearer was
Than things seen in a looking-glass.
Like an old pedlar with his pack,
As light as air upon his back —
His story finished, through and through,
Its scenes still sweet in memory, too,
He'd shut his book, a moment sit,
Inwardly musing over it,
Then stretch his legs, forsake his seat,
Blink his bright eyes, glance up and see
Perhaps a flower, bird, or bee,
Or green leaves dancing in a tree —
Would stand an instant, mute and dazed,
Then out he'd run, as if half-crazed,
Shouting and leaping with delight;
Yes, even at the commonest sight —
Hedgerow in leaf, or finch on twig,
As glad and merry as a grig.
He loved to lie, his daydream eye
Fixed on a blue, or starry sky,
Watching the clouds, or listening
To every note a wren can sing,

To every caw a rook can caw,
Ravished at what he heard and saw —
The green of moss, a radiant drop
Of water in a bramble-cup.
Which pleased him most no tongue could tell—
To look or listen, taste or smell! . . .

This seems to me at least to hint,
That if we give what wits we have
To Books, as Jack himself them gave —
To all we read a willing slave —
The while we dream, delight, and think,
The words a precious meat and drink,
And keep as lively as a spink,
There's not much harm in printer's ink.

THE BOOKWORM

" I'm tired — oh, tired of books," said Jack,
    " I long for meadows green,
And woods where shadowy violets
    Nod their cool leaves between;
I long to see the ploughman stride
    His darkening acres o'er,
To hear the hoarse sea-waters drive
    Their billows 'gainst the shore;
I long to watch the sea-mew wheel
    Back to her rock-perched mate;
Or, where the breathing cows are housed,
    Lean, dreaming, at the gate.
Something has gone, and ink and print
    Will never bring it back;
I long for the green fields again,
    I'm tired of books," said Jack.

TARTARY

If I were Lord of Tartary,
    Myself, and me alone,
My bed should be of ivory,
    Of beaten gold my throne;
And in my court should peacocks flaunt,
And in my forests tigers haunt,
And in my pools great fishes slant
        Their fins athwart the sun.

If I were Lord of Tartary,
    Trumpeters every day
To all my meals should summon me,
    And in my courtyards bray;
And in the evening lamps should shine,
Yellow as honey, red as wine,
While harp, and flute, and mandoline
        Made music sweet and gay.

If I were Lord of Tartary,
    I'd wear a robe of beads,
White, and gold, and green they'd be —
    And small and thick as seeds;
And ere should wane the morning star,
I'd don my robe and scimitar,
And zebras seven should draw my car
        Through Tartary's dark glades.

Lord of the fruits of Tartary,
    Her rivers silver-pale!
Lord of the hills of Tartary,
    Glen, thicket, wood, and dale!
Her flashing stars, her scented breeze,
Her trembling lakes, like foamless seas,
Her bird-delighting citron-trees,
        In every purple vale!

THE SONG OF FINIS

At the edge of All the Ages
    A Knight sate on his steed,
His armour red and thin with rust,
    His soul from sorrow freed;
And he lifted up his visor
    From a face of skin and bone,
And his horse turned head and whinnied
    As the twain stood there alone.

No Bird above that steep of time
    Sang of a livelong quest;
No wind breathed,
        Rest:
" Lone for an end! " cried Knight to steed,
    Loosed an eager rein —
Charged with his challenge into Space:
    And quiet did quiet remain.

NOON

Few and faint a bird's small notes
Stirred on the air and died away
Among the wind-enticing leaves;
And everywhere the crimson may
Lapped in the sun-sweet silence bloomed;
And, lost in lovely reverie,
A mirrored swan upon a pool
Floated beneath a willow tree.

[231]

Moon and
Stars—Night
and Dream

BLAISDELL

SUMMER EVENING

The sandy cat by the Farmer's chair
Mews at his knee for dainty fare;
Old Rover in his moss-greened house
Mumbles a bone, and barks at a mouse.
In the dewy fields the cattle lie
Chewing the cud 'neath a fading sky;
Dobbin at manger pulls his hay:
Gone is another summer's day.

SUPPER

I supped where bloomed the red red rose,
    And a bird in the tree
Looked on my sweet white bread and whistled
    Tunes to me.

And a wasp prowled in the evening light,
    My honey all about;
And the martin to her sun-baked nest
    Swept in and out.

I sat so still in the garden
    That wasp and leaf and bird
Seemed as I dreamed the only things
    That had ever stirred.

MRS. MACQUEEN

With glass like a bull's-eye,
    And shutters of green,
Down on the cobbles
    Lives Mrs. MacQueen.

At six she rises;
    At nine you see
Her candle shine out
    In the linden tree;

And at half-past nine
    Not a sound is nigh,
But the bright moon's creeping
    Across the sky;

Or a far dog baying;
    Or a twittering bird
In its drowsy nest,
    In the darkness stirred;

Or like the roar
    Of a distant sea,
A long-drawn *S-s-sh!*
    In the linden tree.

NIGHTFALL

The last light fails — that shallow pool of day!
The coursers of the dark stamp down to drink,
Arch their wild necks, lift their wild heads and neigh;
Their drivers, gathering at the water-brink,
With eyes ashine from out their clustering hair,
Utter their hollow speech, or gaze afar,
Rapt in irradiant reverie, to where
Languishes, lost in light, the evening star.
Come the wood-nymphs to dance within the glooms,
Calling these charioteers with timbrels' din;
Ashen with twilight the dark forest looms
O'er the nocturnal beasts that prowl within.
" O glory of beauty which the world makes fair! "
Pant they their serenading on the air.

Sound the loud hooves, and all abroad the sky
The lusty charioteers their stations take;
Planet to planet do the sweet Loves fly,
And in the zenith silver music wake.
Cities of men, in blindness hidden low,
Fume their faint flames to that arched firmament,
But all the dwellers in the lonely know
The unearthly are abroad, and weary and spent,
With rush extinguished, to their dreaming go.
And world and night and star-enclustered space
The glory of beauty are in one enravished face.

THE RAVEN'S TOMB

" Build me my tomb," the Raven said,
" Within the dark yew-tree,
So in the Autumn yewberries,
Sad lamps, may burn for me,
Summon the haunted beetle,

[237]

From twilight bud and bloom,
To drone a gloomy dirge for me
At dusk above my tomb.
Beseech ye too the glow-worm
To rear her cloudy flame,
Where the small, flickering bats resort,
Whistling in tears my name.
Let the round dew a whisper make,
Welling on twig and thorn;
And only the grey cock at night
Call through his silver horn.
And you, dear sisters, don your black
For ever and a day,
To show how true a raven
In his tomb is laid away."

BEWARE!

An ominous bird sang from its branch
   " Beware, O Wanderer!
Night 'mid her flowers of glamourie spilled
   Draws swiftly near:

" Night with her darkened caravans,
   Piled deep with silver and myrrh,
Draws from the portals of the East,
   O Wanderer near.

" Night who walks plumèd through the fields
   Of stars that strangely stir —
Smitten to fire by the sandals of him
   Who walks with her."

THE NIGHT-SWANS

'Tis silence on the enchanted lake,
And silence in the air serene,
Save for the beating of her heart,
The lovely-eyed Evangeline.

She sings across the waters clear
And dark with trees and stars between,
The notes her fairy godmother
Taught her, the child Evangeline.

As might the unrippled pool reply,
Faltering an answer far and sweet,
Three swans as white as mountain snow
Swim mantling to her feet.

And still upon the lake they stay,
Their eyes black stars in all their snow,
And softly, in the glassy pool,
Their feet beat darkly to and fro.

She rides upon her little boat,
Her swans swim through the starry sheen,
Rowing her into Fairyland —
The lovely-eyed Evangeline.

'Tis silence on the enchanted lake,
And silence in the air serene;
Voices shall call in vain again
On earth the child Evangeline.

" Evangeline! Evangeline! "
Upstairs, downstairs, all in vain.
Her room is dim; her flowers faded;
She answers not again.

VOICES

Who is it calling by the darkened river
    Where the moss lies smooth and deep,
And the dark trees lean unmoving arms,
    Silent and vague in sleep,
And the bright-heeled constellations pass
    In splendour through the gloom;
Who is it calling o'er the darkened river
    In music, " Come!"?

Who is it wandering in the summer meadows
    Where the children stoop and play
In the green faint-scented flowers, spinning
    The guileless hours away?
Who touches their bright hair? who puts
    A wind-shell to each cheek,
Whispering betwixt its breathing silences,
    " Seek! Seek!"?

Who is it watching in the gathering twilight
    When the curfew bird hath flown
On eager wings, from song to silence,
    To its darkened nest alone?
Who takes for brightening eyes the stars,
    For locks the still moonbeam,
Sighs through the dews of evening peacefully
    Falling, " Dream!"

THE HORSEMAN

I heard a horseman
    Ride over the hill;
The moon shone clear,
    The night was still;

His helm was silver,
    And pale was he;
And the horse he rode
    Was of ivory.

OLD SHELLOVER

" Come! " said Old Shellover.
"What? " says Creep.
" The horny old Gardener's fast asleep;
The fat cock Thrush
To his nest has gone;
And the dew shines bright
In the rising Moon;
Old Sallie Worm from her hole doth peep:
Come! " said Old Shellover.
" Aye! " said Creep.

EEKA, NEEKA

Eeka, Neeka, Leeka, Lee —
Here's a lock without a key;
Bring a lantern, bring a candle,
Here's a door without a handle;
Shine, shine, you old thief Moon,
Here's a door without a room;
Not a whisper, moth or mouse,
Key — lock — door — room: where's the house?

Say nothing, creep away,
And live to knock another day!

THE MAGNIFYING GLASS

With this round glass
I can make *Magic* talk —
A myriad shells show
In a scrap of chalk;

Of but an inch of moss
A forest — flowers and trees;
A drop of water
Like a hive of bees.

I lie in wait and watch
How the deft spider jets
The woven web-silk
From his spinnerets;

The tigerish claws he has!
And oh! the silly flies
That stumble into his net —
With all those eyes!

Not even the tiniest thing
But this my glass
Will make more marvellous,
And itself surpass.

Yes, and with lenses like it,
Eyeing the moon,
'Twould seem you'd walk there
In an afternoon!

THE SHADOW

When the last of gloaming's gone,
When the world is drowned in Night,
Then swims up the great round Moon,
Washing with her borrowed light
Twig, stone, grass-blade — pin-point bright —
Every tiniest thing in sight.

Then, on tiptoe,
Off go I
To a white-washed
Wall near by,

Where, for secret
Company,
My small shadow
Waits for me.

Still and stark,
Or stirring — *so,*
All I'm doing
He'll do too.

Quieter than
A cat he mocks

My walk, my gestures,
Clothes and looks.

I twist and turn,
I creep, I prowl,
Likewise does he,
The crafty soul,
The Moon for lamp,
And for music, owl.

" *Sst!* " I whisper,
" Shadow, come! "
No answer:
He is blind and dumb —
Blind and dumb.

And when I go,
The wall will stand empty,
White as snow.

THE HARE

In the black furrow of a field
I saw an old witch-hare this night;
And she cocked a lissome ear,
And she eyed the moon so bright,
And she nibbled of the green;
And I whispered "Whsst! witch-hare,"
Away like a ghostie o'er the field
She fled, and left the moonlight there.

TIRED TIM

Poor tired Tim! It's sad for him.
He lags the long bright morning through,
Ever so tired of nothing to do;
He moons and mopes the livelong day,
Nothing to think about, nothing to say;
Up to bed with his candle to creep,
Too tired to yawn, too tired to sleep:
Poor tired Tim! It's sad for him.

TO BED

Candle lank and lean and pale
Light me to bed,
Rearing aloft thy flaming hair
Above thy head.

Red is the tip of thy long nose;
As if from weeping
Tears that shall in the night congeal
When I am sleeping.

Up, up the peevish stair we go;
Silent as death
Thy smoke trails back along the air
Like frosty breath.

Circling around thy tapering head
Pale colours bloom,
While shadows watch thee from their lair
Of ghostly gloom.

At every wink they crouch and spring —
I conjure thee
Droop not a languid eyelid till
In bed I be.

And while the mice make romping stir,
I do intreat
Twine not thy spectral body with
A winding sheet.

But steadfast as a sentinel,
Vigilant, stark,
Guard thou the battlements of light
Against the dark!

A LANTERN

A lantern lighted me to bed
        Because I had no candle;
Across the frozen fields it shone
        And danced upon the Wandle.

Cock robin in the icy hedge,
        Nor blackbird, bill in feather,
Nor snail tucked snug in close-shut house
        Will ever now know whether

A lantern lighted me to bed,
        Because I had no candle,
And from my frozen window-pane
        Beamed clean across the Wandle.

THE UNIVERSE

I heard a little child beneath the stars
        Talk as he ran along
To some small riddle in his mind that seemed
        A-tiptoe into song.

In his dark eyes lay a wild universe —
    Wild forests, peaks, and crests;
Angels and fairies, giants, wolves and he
    Were that world's only guests.

Elsewhere was home and mother, his warm bed:
    Now, only God alone
Could, armed with all His power and wisdom, make
    Earths richer than his own.

O Man! — thy dreams, thy passions, hopes, desires! —
    He in his pity keep
A homely bed where love may lull a child's
    Fond Universe asleep!

HIDE AND SEEK

Hide and seek, says the Wind,
    In the shade of the woods;
Hide and seek, says the Moon,
    To the hazel buds;
Hide and seek, says the Cloud,
    Star on to star;

Hide and seek, says the Wave
    At the harbour bar;
Hide and seek, say I,
    To myself, and step
Out of the dream of Wake
    Into the dream of Sleep.

HARK!

My little Charles is afraid of the dark;
Stares at the window, stiff and stark,
Sits up in bed, with tousled head,
White as chalk, scarce able to talk. . . .
    " *Listen!* " he whispers; "*Hark!* " . . .

" My dear, my dear, my dear, my *dear*!
See, you are safe; just us.
It's only the wind at the keyhole,
It's only a nibbling mouse;

[246]

Only the creak of an empty stair;
And the moon looking into the house;
It's only a moth on the ceiling;
Or a little screech owl in the wood.
There's nothing behind the door ajar.
Stop breathing as long as you could,
You still wouldn't hear what you think you hear;
There's nothing to fear in what you fear —
    Lying alone in the dark."

Poor little Charles, he weeps at me;
Begs and prays he may sleep with me;
Tear-dabbled cheeks, wild eyes I see;
And a silence falls in the vacancy. . . .

   " Listen! . . ." he whispers. *" Hark! . . ."*

MANY A MICKLE

A little sound —
Only a little, a little —
The breath in a reed,
A trembling fiddle;
A trumpet's ring,
The shuddering drum;
So all the glory, bravery, hush
Of music come.

A little sound —
Only a stir and a sigh
Of each green leaf
Its fluttering neighbour by;
Oak on to oak,
The wide dark forest through —
So o'er the watery wheeling world
The night winds go.

A little sound,
Only a little, a little —
The thin high drone
Of the simmering kettle,
The gathering frost,
The click of needle and thread;
Mother, the fading wall, the dream,
The drowsy bed.

SONG

O for a moon to light me home!
   O for a lanthorn green!
For those sweet stars the Pleiades,
That glitter in the twilight trees;
   O for a lovelorn taper! O
   For a lanthorn green!

O for a frock of tartan!
   O for clear, wild, grey eyes!
For fingers light as violets,
'Neath branches that the blackbird frets;
   O for a thistly meadow! O
   For clear, wild, grey eyes!

O for a heart like almond boughs!
   O for sweet thoughts like rain!
O for first-love like fields of grey,
Shut April-buds at break of day!
   O for a sleep like music!
   Dreams still as rain!

THE FLEETING

The late wind failed; high on the hill
The pines' resounding boughs were still.
The wondrous airs that space had lent
To wail earth's nightlong banishment
From heat and light and song of day
In a last sighing died away.

Alone in that muteness, lost and small,
I watched from sickled Leo fall
An ebbing trail of silvery dust.
Yet, fixed in station, near and far,
Giittered in quiet star to star;
And dreamed in midnight's dim immense
Heaven's universal innocence.

O transient heart, that yet can raise
To the unseen its pang of praise,
And from the founts in play above
Be freshed with that sweet love!

LULLY

Nay, ninny, shut those sleepy eyes,
    The robin from his spray
Long since to his cold winter roost
    Has flown away.

Hush, now, and fold those gentle hands;
    Across the fields the snow
Has hidden the bleating sheep from sight,
    And heaped the hedges through.

Wail not so shrill, thou tiny voice;
    These shadows mean no harm;

'Tis but the flames this wintry night
    To keep thee safe and warm;
Lully, and rest then, pretty soul,
    Safe on thy mother's arm.

LULLABY

Sleep, sleep, thou lovely one!
The little mouse cheeps plaintively,
The nightingale in the chestnut-tree —
They sing together, bird and mouse,
In starlight, in darkness, lonely, sweet,
The wild notes and the faint notes meet —
    Sleep, sleep, thou lovely one!

Sleep, sleep, thou lovely one!
Amid the lilies floats the moth,
The mole along his galleries goeth
In the dark earth; the summer moon
Looks like a shepherd through the pane
Seeking his feeble lamb again —
    Sleep, sleep, thou lovely one!

Sleep, sleep, thou lovely one!
Time comes to keep night-watch with thee,
Nodding with roses, and the sea
Saith " Peace! Peace! " amid his foam.
" O be still! "
The wind cries up the whispering hill —
    Sleep, sleep, thou lovely one!

SHE IN THY DREAMS WATCH OVER THEE!

She in thy dreams watch over thee!
Who in the dark and cold
Keeps all her buds of earth fast-sealed,
Her meek sheep safe in fold;
Who comes with dew and goes with dew;
And lulls the winds to rest;
And hushes the weary birds of eve
To silence on her breast.

She of the ages of the night,
The childhood of the morn,
Solace the sadness of thy thoughts
Long waking made forlorn;
Stoop with the stillness of her smile,
The safety of her hand,
Charm with the clear call of her voice,
Thee, in the shadowy land!

The daisy will unfold in light
The fairness of her face,
The lark from his green furrow course
Back to his sun-wild place;
Then she, whose drowsy cheek by thine
Lonely all night hath lain,
Will toss her dark locks from thy sweet eyes,
Loose thee to earth again!

I MET AT EVE

I met at eve the Prince of Sleep
His was a still and lovely face,
He wandered through a valley steep,
Lovely in a lonely place.

His garb was grey of lavender,
About his brows a poppy-wreath
Burned like dim coals, and everywhere
    The air was sweeter for his breath.

His twilight feet no sandals wore,
His eyes shone faint in their own flame,
Fair moths that gloomed his steps before
    Seemed letters of his lovely name.

His house is in the mountain ways,
A phantom house of misty walls,
Whose golden flocks at evening graze,
    And 'witch the moon with muffled calls.

Upwelling from his shadowy springs
Sweet waters shake a trembling sound,
There flit the hoot-owl's silent wings,
    There hath his web the silkworm wound.

Dark in his pools clear visions lurk,
And rosy, as with morning buds,
Along his dales of broom and birk
    Dreams haunt his solitary woods.

I met at eve the Prince of Sleep,
His was a still and lovely face,
He wandered through a valley steep,
    Lovely in a lonely place.

ASLEEP

Sister with sister, dark and fair,
Slumber on one pillow there;
Tranced in dream their phantoms rove —
But none knows what they are dreaming of.
Lost to the room they love, they lie
Their hearts their only lullaby.
Whither that cloud in heaven is bound
Can neither tell. No scent, no sound
Reaches them now. Without avail
Warbles the sweet-tongued nightingale.
Oh, how round, how white a moon
Streams into this silent room!
Clothes and curtains gleam so gay
    It might be day.
But see, beyond that door ajar,
    Night's shadows are;
And not a mouse is stirring where
    Descends an empty stair.

SILVER

Slowly, silently, now the moon
Walks the night in her silver shoon;

This way, and that, she peers, and sees
Silver fruit upon silver trees;
One by one the casements catch
Her beams beneath the silvery thatch;
Couched in his kennel, like a log,
With paws of silver sleeps the dog;
From their shadowy cote the white breasts peep
Of doves in a silver-feathered sleep;
A harvest mouse goes scampering by,
With silver claws, and silver eye;
And moveless fish in the water gleam,
By silver reeds in a silver stream.

DREAM–SONG

Sunlight, moonlight,
Twilight, starlight —
Gloaming at the close of day,
And an owl calling,
Cool dews falling
In a wood of oak and may.

Lantern-light, taper-light,
Torch-light, no-light:
Darkness at the shut of day,
And lions roaring,
Their wrath pouring
In wild waste places far away.

Elf-light, bat-light,
Touchwood-light and toad-light,
And the sea a shimmering gloom of grey,
And a small face smiling
In a dream's beguiling
In a world of wonders far away.

THE UNFINISHED DREAM

Rare-sweet the air in that unimagined country —
    My spirit had wandered far
From its weary body close-enwrapt in slumber
    Where its home and earth-friends are;

A milk-like air — and of light all abundance;
    And there a river clear
Painting the scene like a picture on its bosom,
    Green foliage drifting near.

No sign of life I saw, as I pressed onward,
    Fish, nor beast, nor bird,
Till I came to a hill clothed in flowers to its summit,
    Then shrill small voices I heard.

And I saw from concealment a company of elf-folk
    With faces strangely fair,
Talking their unearthly scattered talk together,
    A bind of green-grasses in their hair,

Marvellously gentle, feater far than children,
    In gesture, mien and speech,
Hastening onward in translucent shafts of sunshine,
    And gossiping each with each.

Straw-light their locks, on neck and shoulder falling,
    Faint of almond the silks they wore,
Spun not of worm, but as if inwoven of moonbeams
    And foam on rock-bound shore;

Like lank-legged grasshoppers in June-tide meadows,
    Amalillios of the day,
Hungrily gazed upon by me — a stranger,
    In unknown regions astray.

Yet, happy beyond words, I marked their sunlit faces,
　　Stealing soft enchantment from their eyes,
Tears in my own confusing their small image,
　　Harkening their bird-like cries.

They passed me, unseeing, a waft of flocking linnets;
　　Sadly I fared on my way;
And came in my dream to a dreamlike habitation,
　　Close-shut, festooned and grey.

Pausing, I gazed at the porch dust-still, vine-wreathèd,
　　Worn the stone steps thereto,
Mute hung its bell, whence a stony head looked downward,
　　Grey 'gainst the sky's pale-blue —

Strange to me: Strange . . .

RAIN

I woke in the swimming dark
And heard, now sweet, now shrill,
The voice of the rain-water,
　　Cold and still,

Endlessly sing; now faint,
In the distance borne away;
Now in the air float near,
　　But nowhere stay;

Singing I know not what,
Echoing on and on;
Following me in sleep,
　　Till night was gone.

THE HOUSE OF DREAM

Candle, candle, burning clear,
Now the House of Dream draws near;
See what shadowy flowers move
The solitary porch above;
Hark, how still it is within,
Though so many guests go in.

No faint voice will answer make
While thy tapering flame's awake.
Candle, candle, burning low,
It is time for me to go.
Music, faint and distant, wells
From those far-off dales and dells.

Now in shoes of silence I
Stand by the walls of witchery;
Out then, earthly flame, for see,
Sleep's unlatched her door to me.

FULL MOON

One night as Dick lay fast asleep,
    Into his drowsy eyes
A great still light began to creep
    From out the silent skies.
It was the lovely moon's, for when
    He raised his dreamy head,
Her surge of silver filled the pane
    And streamed across his bed.
So, for awhile, each gazed at each —
    Dick and the solemn moon —
Till, climbing slowly on her way,
    She vanished, and was gone.

[257]

ECHO

Seven sweet notes
In the moonlight pale
Warbled a leaf-hidden
Nightingale:
And Echo in hiding
By an old green wall
Under the willows
Sighed back them all.

WANDERERS

Wide are the meadows of night,
And daisies are shining there,
Tossing their lovely dews,
Lustrous and fair;
And through these sweet fields go,
Wand'rers 'mid the stars —
Venus, Mercury, Uranus, Neptune,
Saturn, Jupiter, Mars.

'Tired in their silver, they move,
And circling, whisper and say,
Fair are the blossoming meads of delight
Through which we stray.

STARS

If to the heavens you lift your eyes
When Winter reigns o'er our Northern skies,
And snow-cloud none the zenith mars,
At Yule-tide midnight these your stars:
Low in the South see bleak-blazing Sirius;
Above him hang Betelgeuse, Procyon wan;

Wild-eyed to West of him, Rigel and Bellatrix,
And rudd-red Aldebaran journeying on.
High in night's roof-tree beams twinkling Capella;
Vega and Deneb prowl low in the North;
Far to the East roves the Lion-heart, Regulus;
While the twin sons of Zeus to'rd the zenith gleam forth.

But when Midsummer Eve in man's sleep-drowsed hours
Refreshes for daybreak its dew-bright flowers,
Though three of these Night Lights aloft remain,
For nine, if you gaze, you will gaze in vain.
Yet comfort find, for, far-shining there,
See golden Arcturus and cold Altaïr;
Crystalline Spica, and, strange to scan,
Blood-red Antares, foe to Man.

WILL EVER?

Will he ever be weary of wandering,
    The flaming sun?
Ever weary of waning in lovelight,
    The white still moon?
Will ever a shepherd come
    With a crook of simple gold,
And lead all the little stars
    Like lambs to the fold?

Will ever the Wanderer sail
    From over the sea,
Up the river of water,
    To the stones to me?
Will he take us all into his ship,
    Dreaming, and waft us far,
To where in the clouds of the West
    The Islands are?

Odds
and
Ends

MIMA

Jemima is my name,
    But oh, I have another;
My father always calls me Meg,
    And so do Bob and mother;
Only my sister, jealous of
    The strands of my bright hair,
" Jemima — Mima — Mima! "
    Calls, mocking, up the stair.

ALAS, ALACK!

Ann, Ann!
    Come! quick as you can!
There's a fish that *talks*
    In the frying-pan.
Out of the fat,
    As clear as glass,
He put up his mouth
    And moaned " Alas! "
Oh, most mournful,
    " Alas, alack! "
Then turned to his sizzling,
    And sank him back.

THERE WAS AN OLD WOMAN

There was an old Woman of Bumble Bhosey —
    Children she had forty;
Half of them sang hymns all night;
    Half of them were naughty;
Twenty went to Botany Bay;
    Ten of them on crutches,
And the last of them nimmed the clouts that lay
    A-bleaching on the bushes!

BLINDMAN'S IN

" *Applecumjockaby,* blindfold eye!
How many rooks come sailing by,
Caw — caw, in the deep blue sky? "

" *Applecumjockaby, you* tell me!
I can listen though I can't see;
Twenty soot-black rooks there be."

" *Applecumjockaby,* I say, No!
Who can tell what he don't know?
Blindman's in, and round we go."

BLACKBIRDS

In April, when these orchards blow,
The boughs are white as driven snow.
Dark-leafed in May, like beads are seen
Hard little berries of a bright clear green.
A rosy flush steals through the skin,
While the small almond kernel swells within.
The Sun pours down his golden rain;
And soon comes honeyed June again:
Listen! — the Wood-boy's drowsy flute! —
Or is it some wild blackbird in the ripe red fruit?

QUACK!

The duck is whiter than whey is,
His tail tips up over his back,
The eye in his head is as round as a button,
And he says, *Quack! Quack!*

He swims on his bright blue mill-pond,
By the willow tree under the shack,
Then stands on his head to see down to the bottom,
And says, *Quack! Quack!*

When Mollie steps out of the kitchen,
For apron — pinned round with a sack;
He squints at her round face, her dish, and what's in it,
And says, *Quack! Quack!*

He preens the pure snow of his feathers
In the sun by the wheat-straw stack;
At dusk waddles home with his brothers and sisters,
And says, *Quack! Quack!*

JIM JAY

Do diddle di do,
   Poor Jim Jay
Got stuck fast
   In Yesterday.
Squinting he was,
   On cross-legs bent,
Never heeding
   The wind was spent.
Round veered the weathercock,
   The sun drew in —
And stuck was Jim
   Like a rusty pin. . . .

We pulled and we pulled
   From seven till twelve,
Jim, too frightened
   To help himself.
But all in vain.
   The clock struck one,
And there was Jim
   A little bit gone.
At half-past five
   You scarce could see
A glimpse of his flapping
   Handkerchee.

And when came noon,
　　And we climbed sky-high,
Jim was a speck
　　Slip — slipping by.

Come to-morrow,
　　The neighbours say,
He'll be past crying for:
　　Poor Jim Jay.

" SOOEEP! "

Black as a chimney is his face,
And ivory white his teeth,
And in his brass-bound cart he rides,
The chestnut blooms beneath.

" Sooeep, Sooeep! " he cries, and brightly peers
This way and that, to see
With his two light-blue shining eyes
What custom there may be.

And once inside the house, he'll squat,
And drive his rods on high,
Till twirls his sudden sooty brush
Against the morning sky.

Then, 'mid his bulging bags of soot,
With half the world asleep,
His small cart wheels him off again,
Still hoarsely bawling, " Sooeep! "

A — APPLE PIE

Little Pollie Pillikins
Peeped into the kitchen,
" H'm," says she, " Ho," says she,
　　" Nobody there! "
Only little meeny mice,
Miniken and miching
On the big broad flagstones, empty and bare.

Greedy Pollie Pillikins
Crept into the pantry,
There stood an Apple Pasty,
    Sugar white as snow.
Off the shelf she toppled it,
Quick and quiet and canty,
And the meeny mice they watched her
    On her tip-tap-toe.

" Thief, Pollie Pillikins! "
Crouching in the shadows there,
Flickering in the candle-shining,
    Fee, fo, fum!
Munching up the pastry,
Crunching up the apples,
" Thief! " squeaked the smallest mouse,
    " Pollie, spare a crumb! "

POOR HENRY

Thick in its glass
    The physic stands,
Poor Henry lifts
    Distracted hands;
His round cheek wans
    In the candlelight,
To smell that smell!
    To see that sight!

Finger and thumb
    Clinch his small nose,
A gurgle, a gasp,
    And down it goes;
Scowls Henry now;
    But mark that cheek,
Sleek with the bloom
    Of health next week!

LOB–LIE–BY–THE–FIRE

Keep me a crust
Or starve I must;
Hoard me a bone
Or I am gone;
A handful of coals
Leave red for me;
Or the smouldering log
Of a wild-wood tree;

Even a kettle
To sing on the hob
Will comfort the heart
Of poor old Lob:
Then with his hairy
Hands he'll bless
Prosperous master,
And kind mistress.

GRIM

Beside the blaze, as of forty fires,
Giant Grim doth sit,
Roasting a thick-woolled mountain sheep
Upon an iron spit.
Above him wheels the winter sky,
Beneath him, fathoms deep,
Lies hidden in the valley mists
A village fast asleep —
Save for one restive hungry dog
That, snuffing towards the height,
Smells Grim's broiled supper-meat, and spies
His watch-fire twinkling bright.

THE LITTLE OLD CUPID

'Twas a very small garden;
The paths were of stone,
Scattered with leaves,
With moss overgrown;
And a little old Cupid
Stood under a tree,
With a small broken bow
He stood aiming at me.

The dog-rose in briers
Hung over the weeds,
The air was aflock
With the floating of seeds;
And a little old Cupid
Stood under a tree,
With a small broken bow
He stood aiming at me.

The dovecote was tumbling,
The fountain dry,
A wind in the orchard
Went whispering by;
And a little old Cupid
Stood under a tree,
With a small broken bow
He stood aiming at me.

THE TENT

How cool a tent!
How leafy a shade!
And, near at hand, a heap of sticks.
The kettle waits,
The cloth is laid —
With fruit and bread and Banbury cakes.
Cows rove the meadows; in woods afar
Steals out a listening fox:
I wonder where the campers are,
And what is in that box.

MISS T.

It's a very odd thing —
    As odd as can be —
That whatever Miss T. eats
    Turns into Miss T.;
Porridge and apples,
    Mince, muffins and mutton,
Jam, junket, jumbles —
    Not a rap, not a button

It matters; the moment
    They're out of her plate,
Though shared by Miss Butcher
    And sour Mr. Bate;
Tiny and cheerful,
    And neat as can be,
Whatever Miss T. eats
    Turns into Miss T.

FOR MOPSA

Ah, would I were a Pastrycook!
My Mopsa then I'd make
A Sallie Lunn, a Crumpet, and a
    Cake.

Ah, would I were a Grocer!
How happy she should be
With Jars of Honey, Raisins, Currants,
    Tea.

Ah, would I were an Oilman!
She should never, never mope
For Clothes Pegs, Candles, Soda, or for
    Soap.

Ah, would I were a Pothecary!
For Possets she'd not pine,
Or Pills, or Ipecacuanha
    Wine.

Or, just suppose, a Fishmonger!
The *pains* I would be at
To pick her out a Whitebait, or a
    Sprat!

Or a green-baize-aproned Fruiterer —
The punnets that should come
Of Cherries, Apples, Peach, and Pear, and
    Plum!

There's a small dark shop I know of too,
In another place, called Sleep;
And there's nothing sold in Dreams it doesn't
    Keep.

But as it's only rhymes I make,
I can but dower my Dove
With scribbles, and with kisses, and with
    Love.

MISS CHERRY

Once — once I loved:
And Miss Cherry was she
Who took my heart captive,
And set my heart free.

I'd sing, and I'd sing
What no words ever meant,
And never felt lonely
Wherever I went.

No bird in the air,
No fish in the sea,
No skylark in heaven
Could happier be.

Never hungry or tired,
From breakfast to bed;
I just nibbled, and thought
Of Miss Cherry instead.

All night I would sleep
Like a top, until day
With a shower of sunbeams
Washed slumber away.

And it seemed that the World
Was a Wonder to see,
Since I loved Miss Cherry,
And Miss Cherry loved me.

THE APPLE CHARM

I plucked an apple, sleek and red,
I took his three black pips,
Stuck two upon my cheek, and brow,
And t'other on my lips.

Dick on my cheek, the other Tom,
But O — my love to be —
Robin that couched upon my lip
Was truest unto me.

KIPH

My Uncle Ben, who's been
To Bisk, Bhir, Biak —
Been, and come back:
To Tab, Tau, Tze, and Tomsk,
And home, by Teneriffe:
Who, brown as desert sand,
Gaunt, staring, slow and stiff,
Has chased the Unicorn
And Hippogriff,
Gave me a smooth, small, shining stone,
Called *Kiph*.

"Look'ee, now, Nevvy mine,"
He told me — "*If*
You'd wish a wish,
Just rub this smooth, small, shining stone,
Called *Kiph*."

Hide it did I,
In a safe, secret spot;
Slept, and the place
In dreams forgot.

One wish *alone*
Now's mine: Oh, if
I could but find again
That stone called *Kiph!*

Somewhere

BLAISDELL

THE LITTLE BIRD

My dear Daddie bought a mansion
    For to bring my Mammie to,
In a hat with a long feather,
    And a trailing gown of blue;
And a company of fiddlers
    And a rout of maids and men
Danced the clock round to the morning,
    In a gay house-warming then.
And when all the guests were gone — and
    All was still as still can be,
In from the dark ivy hopped a
    Wee small bird. And that was Me.

"POOR BIRD"

Poor bird! —
No hands, no fingers thine;
Two angel-coloured wings instead:
But where are mine?

Cold voiceless fish! —
No hands, no spindly legs, no toes;
But fins and a tail,
And a mouth for nose.

Wild weed! —
Not even an eye with which to see!
Or ear, or tongue,
For sigh or song;
Or heart to beat,
Or mind to long.

And yet — ah, would that I,
In sun and shade, like thee,
Might no less gentle, sweet,
And lovely be!

ME

As long as I live
I shall always be
My Self — and no other,
Just me.

Like a tree —
Willow, elder,
Aspen, thorn,
Or cypress forlorn.

Like a flower,
For its hour —

Primrose, or pink,
Or a violet —
Sunned by the sun,
And with dewdrops wet.

Always just me.
Till the day come on
When I leave this body,
It's all then done,
And the spirit within it
Is gone.

THE CHRISTENING

The bells chime clear,
Soon will the sun behind the hills sink down;
Come, little Ann, your baby brother dear
Lies in his christening-gown.

His godparents
Are all across the fields stepped on before,
And wait beneath the crumbling monuments,
This side the old church door.

Your mammie dear
Leans frail and lovely on your daddie's arm;
Watching her chick, 'twixt happiness and fear,
Lest he should come to harm.

All to be blest
Full soon in the clear heavenly water, he
Sleeps on unwitting of't, his little breast
Heaving so tenderly.

[276]

I carried you,
My little Ann, long since on this same quest,
And from the painted windows a pale hue
Lit golden on your breast;

And then you woke,
Chill as the holy water trickled down,
And, weeping, cast the window a strange look,
Half smile, half infant frown.

I scarce could hear
The skylarks singing in the green meadows,
'Twas summertide, and, budding far and near,
The hedges thick with rose.

And now you're grown
A little girl; and this same helpless mite
Is come like such another bud half-blown,
Out of the wintry night.

Time flies, time flies!
And yet, bless me! 'tis little changed am I;
May Jesu keep from tears those infant eyes,
Be love their lullaby!

TWO DEEP CLEAR EYES

Two deep clear eyes,
Two ears, a mouth, a nose,
Ten supple fingers,
And ten nimble toes,
Two hands, two feet, two arms, two legs,
And a heart through which love's blessing flows.

Eyes bid ears
Hark:
Ears bid eyes
Mark:
Mouth bids nose
Smell:

Nose says to mouth,
I will:
Heart bids mind
Wonder:
Mind bids heart
Ponder.

Arms, hands, feet, legs,
Work, play, stand, walk;
And a jimp little tongue in a honey-sweet mouth,
With rows of teeth due North and South,
Does nothing but talk, talk, talk.

DREAMLAND

Annie has run to the mill dam,
Annie is down by the weir;
Who was it calling her name, then?
Nobody else to hear?
Cold the water, calm and deep,
Honey-sweet goldilocks half-asleep,
Where the green-grey willows weep,
Annie is down by the weir.

THE DOUBLE

I curtseyed to the dovecote.
I curtseyed to the well.
I twirled me round and round about,
The morning scents to smell.
When out I came from spinning so,
Lo, betwixt green and blue
Was the ghost of me — a fairy child —
A-dancing — dancing, too.

Nought was of her wearing
That is the earth's array.
Her thistledown feet beat airy fleet,
Yet set no blade astray.
The gossamer shining dews of June
Showed grey against the green;
Yet never so much as a bird-claw print
Of footfall to be seen.

Fading in the mounting sun,
That image soon did pine.
Fainter than moonlight thinned the locks
That shone as clear as mine.
Vanished! Vanished! O, sad it is
To spin and spin — in vain;
And never to see the ghost of me
A-dancing there again.

FULL CIRCLE

When thou art as little as I am, Mother,
And I as old as thou,
I'll feed thee on wild-bee honeycomb,
And milk from my cow.
I'll make thee a swan's-down bed, Mother;
Watch over thee then will I.
And if in a far-away dream you start
I'll sing thee lullaby.
It's many — Oh, ages and ages, Mother,
We've shared, we two. Soon, now:
Thou shalt be happy, grown again young,
And I as old as thou.

ALL THE WAY

All the way from Adam
You came, my dear, to me;
The wind upon your cheek
Wafted Noah on the sea,
The daisy in your hand —
Silver petals, stud of gold, —
Just such another starred the grass,
        In Eden, of old.

It's a long, long way to Abel,
And a path of thorns to Cain,
And men less wise than Solomon
Must tread them both again;
But those fountains still are spouting,
And the Serpent twines the bough,
And lovely Eve is sleeping
        In our orchard, *now*.

THE BEAD MAT

We had climbed the last steep flight of stairs;
    Alone were she and I:
" It's something I wanted to give to you,"
    She whispered, with a sigh.

There, in her own small room she stood —
    Where the last beam of sun
Burned in the glass — and showed me what
    For me she had done: —

An oblong shining mat of beads,
    Yellow and white and green,
And where the dark-blue middle was
    A gold between.

I heard no far-off voice, no sound:
    Only her clear grey eyes
Drank in the thoughts that in my face
    Passed shadow-wise.

She clasped her hands, and turned her head,
    And in the watchful glass
She saw how many things had seen
    All that had passed.

She snatched her gift away; her cheek
    With scarlet was aflame;
" It isn't *any*thing," she said,
    " If *we*'re the same! "

Her eyes were like a stormy sea,
    Forlorn, and vast, and grey,
Wherein a little beaten ship
    Flew through the spray.

THE PLAYMATE

Weep no more, nor grieve, nor sigh;
Wet and cold with tears is yet
The saddened lustre of thine eye;
Tears, dear, do darken it.

Weep no more, thy grief hath made
Too wild an autumn for so small
And meek a mouth, and tears have laid
Shadow where they fall.

Weep no more; how dark a face
In thy hair! Oh, I shall see
How many years, this silent place
Where I was cruel to thee!

STRANGERS

The sad bells sound;
Night hastens on apace;
Oh, leave me not to languish
    In this place!

I stand, I know,
Beside you, weeping not,
Pressing my childish Why?
    My stubborn What?

I would forgive
If only a dream you are,
If only a little I'm to stay,
    And wake afar.

Cold is this church,
Cold the high arches, cold
With dazzling light, and Oh,
    How old! how old!

Under the hollow roof
The strangers' voices come —
" The night is dark, and I
    Am far from home."

MUSIC

When music sounds, gone is the earth I know,
And all her lovely things even lovelier grow;
Her flowers in vision flame, her forest trees
Lift burdened branches, stilled with ecstasies.

When music sounds, out of the water rise
Naiads whose beauty dims my waking eyes,
Rapt in strange dreams burns each enchanted face,
With solemn echoing stirs their dwelling-place.

When music sounds, all that I was I am
Ere to this haunt of brooding dust I came;
While from Time's woods break into distant song
The swift-winged hours, as I haste along.

HAUNTED

The rabbit in his burrow keeps
No guarded watch, in peace he sleeps;
The wolf that howls in challenging night
Cowers to her lair at morning light;
The simplest bird entwines a nest
Where she may lean her lovely breast,
Couched in the silence of the bough.
But thou, O man, what rest hast thou?

Thy emptiest solitude can bring
Only a subtler questioning
In thy divided heart. Thy bed
Recalls at dawn what midnight said.
Seek how thou wilt to feign content,
Thy flaming ardour's quickly spent;
Soon thy last company is gone,
And leaves thee — with thyself — alone.

[283]

Pomp and great friends may hem thee round,
A thousand busy tasks be found;
Earth's thronging beauties may beguile
Thy longing lovesick heart awhile;
And pride, like clouds of sunset, spread
A changing glory round thy head;
But fade will all; and thou must come,
Hating thy journey, homeless, home.

Rave how thou wilt; unmoved, remote,
That inward presence slumbers not,
Frets out each secret from thy breast,
Gives thee no rally, pause, nor rest,
Scans close thy very thoughts, lest they
Should sap his patient power away,
Answers thy wrath with peace, thy cry
With tenderest taciturnity.

THE QUIET ENEMY

Hearken! now the hermit bee
Drones a quiet threnody;
Greening on the stagnant pool
The crisscross light is beautiful;
In the venomed yew tree wings
Preen and flit. The linnet sings.

Gradually the brave sun
Sinks to a day's journey done;
In the marshy flats abide
Mists to muffle midnight-tide.
Puffed within the belfry tower
Hungry owls drowse out their hour. . .

Walk in beauty. Vaunt thy rose.
Flaunt thy poisonous loveliness!

Pace for pace with thee there goes
A shape that hath not come to bless.
I, thine enemy? . . . Nay, nay!
I can only watch, and wait
Patient treacherous time away,
Hold ajar the wicket gate.

WHY

" Why do you weep, Mother? Why do you weep?
The evening light has ceased to shine,
  The wind has fallen asleep;
Try as I may, the dreams will come,
  Yet still awake you keep;
Why do you weep, Mother? Why do you weep?

" Why do you sigh, Mother? Why do you sigh?
The world is silent; it is night;
  The stars are in the sky;
No knock would come as late as this,
  No footsteps go by;
I want us now to be alone,
  Just you and I.
Why do you sigh, Mother? Why do you sigh? "

THE FUNERAL

They dressed us up in black,
Susan and Tom and me;
And, walking through the fields
All beautiful to see,
With branches high in the air
And daisy and buttercup,
We heard the lark in the clouds, —
In black dressed up.

They took us to the graves,
Susan and Tom and me,
Where the long grasses grow
And the funeral tree:
We stood and watched; and the wind
Came softly out of the sky
And blew in Susan's hair,
As I stood close by.

Back through the fields we came,
Tom and Susan and me,
And we sat in the nursery together,
And had our tea.
And, looking out of the window,
I heard the thrushes sing;
But Tom fell asleep in his chair.
He was so tired, poor thing.

AT LAST

A mound in a corner,
A sprinkle of snow
To tell how in summer
The daisies will blow;
And a thorn, a bare thorn
Whereto he may flit —
That lone bird, the redbreast,
To whistle on it;
No warmth but the sun's
Brief wintry red ray,
Ere the dark with all heaven
Wheels cold above day.

I shall stay fast asleep —
This poor dust that I am,
In the plentiful earth,
Naked, just as I came;
With all my strange dreams,
Passions, sorrow, delight,
Like the seed of the wild flowers,
Hid deep out of sight;
Like the song of the bird
In the silence of night.

EVER

Ever, ever
Stir and shiver
The reeds and rushes
By the river:
Ever, ever,
As if in dream,

The lone moon's silver
Sleeks the stream.
What old sorrow,
What lost love,
Moon, reeds, rushes,
Dream you of?

BITTER WATERS

In a dense wood, a drear wood,
   Dark water is flowing;
Deep, deep, beyond sounding,
   A flood ever flowing.

There harbours no wild bird,
   No wanderer strays there;
Wreathed in mist, sheds pale Ishtar
   Her sorrowful rays there.

Take thy net; cast thy line;
   Manna sweet be thy baiting;
Time's desolate ages
   Shall still find thee waiting

For quick fish to rise there,
    Or butterfly wooing,
Or flower's honeyed beauty,
    Or wood-pigeon's cooing.

Inland wellsprings are sweet;
    But to lips, parched and dry,
Salt, salt is the savour
    Of these; faint their sigh;

Bitter Babylon's waters!
    Zion, distant and fair!
We hanged up our harps
    On the trees that are there.

NOBODY KNOWS

Often I've heard the Wind sigh
    By the ivied orchard wall,
Over the leaves in the dark night,
    Breathe a sighing call,
And faint away in the silence,
    While I, in my bed,
Wondered, 'twixt dreaming and waking,
    What it said.

Nobody knows what the Wind is,
    Under the height of the sky,
Where the hosts of the stars keep far away house
    And its wave sweeps by —
Just a great wave of the air,
    Tossing the leaves in its sea,
And foaming under the eaves of the roof
    That covers me.

And so we live under deep water,
    All of us, beasts and men,
And our bodies are buried down under the sand,
    When we go again;
And leave, like the fishes, our shells,
    And float on the wind and away,
To where, o'er the marvellous tides of the air,
        Burns day.

AS I DID ROVE

As I did rove in blinded night,
Raying the sward, in slender ring,
A cirque I saw whose crystal light
Tranced my despair with glittering.

Slender its gold; in hues of dream
Its jewels burned, smiting my eyes
Like wings that flit about the stream
That waters Paradise.

Sorrow broke in my heart to see
A thing so lovely; and I heard
Cry from its dark security
A 'wildered bird.

THEY TOLD ME

They told me Pan was dead, but I
    Oft marvelled who it was that sang
Down the green valleys languidly
    Where the grey elder-thickets hang.

Sometimes I thought it was a bird
    My soul had charged with sorcery;
Sometimes it seemed my own heart heard
    Inland the sorrow of the sea.

But even where the primrose sets
    The seal of her pale loveliness,
I found amid the violets
    Tears of an antique bitterness.

THE PATH

Is it an abbey that I see
Hard-by that tapering poplar-tree,
Whereat that path hath end?
'Tis wondrous still
That empty hill,
Yet calls me, friend.

Smooth is the turf, serene the sky,
The time-worn, crumbling roof awry;
Within that turret slim
Hangs there a bell
Whose faint notes knell?
Do colours dim.

Burn in that angled window there,
Grass-green, and crimson, azure rare?
Would, from that narrow door,
One, looking in,
See, gemlike, shine
On walls and floor

Candles whose aureole flames must seem —
So still they burn — to burn in dream?
And do they cry, and say,
" See, stranger; come!
Here is thy home;
No longer stray! "

[290]

DEAR DELIGHT

Youngling fair, and dear delight,
'Tis Love hath thee in keeping;
Green are the hills in morning light,
A long adieu to weeping!

The elfin-folk sing shrill a-ring;
Children a-field are straying;
Dance, too, thou tiny, lovely thing,
For all the world's a-maying.

Droop will the shadows of the night;
Quiet be thy sleeping.
Thou youngling fair, and dear delight,
'Tis Love hath thee in keeping.

GAZE NOW

Gaze, now, thy fill, beguiling face,
Life which all light and hue bestows
Stealeth at last from youth its grace,
From cheek its firstling rose.

Dark are those tresses; grave that brow;
Drink, happy mouth, from Wisdom's well;
Bid the strange world to sigh thee now
All beauty hath to tell.

THE SUNKEN GARDEN

Speak not — whisper not;
Here bloweth thyme and bergamot;
Softly on the evening hour,
Secret herbs their spices shower.

[291]

Dark-spiked rosemary and myrrh,
Lean-stalked purple lavender;
Hides within her bosom, too,
All her sorrows, bitter rue.

Breathe not — trespass not;
Of this green and darkling spot,
Latticed from the moon's beams,
Perchance a distant dreamer dreams;
Perchance upon its darkening air,
The unseen ghosts of children fare,
Faintly swinging, sway and sweep,
Like lovely sea-flowers in its deep;
While, unmoved, to watch and ward,
Amid its gloomed and daisied sward,
Stands with bowed and dewy head
That one little leaden Lad.

ALAS

One moment take thy rest.
Out of mere nought in space
Beauty moved human breast
To tell in this far face
A dream in noonday seen,

Never to fade or pass;
A breath-time's mute delight:
A joy in flight:
The aught desire doth mean,
Sighing, Alas!

INNOCENCY

(*For a Picture*)

In this grave picture mortal Man may see
That all his knowledge ends in mystery.
From mother's womb he breaks. With tortured sighs
Her racked heart sweetens at his angry cries.
Teaching his feet to walk, his tongue to express
His infant love, she pours her tenderness.

[292]

Her milk and honey he doth taste and sip;
Sleeps with her kiss of kindness on his lip.
But with the vigour mastering time doth yield
He exults in freedom; ventures him afield;
Down to the sea goes, and in ship sets sail,
Crazed with the raving of love's nightingale,

And trumps of war, and danger's luring horn,
And dark's faint summons into dreams forlorn.
Pride in earth's vanquished secrets fills his breast;
Yet still he pines for foregone peace and rest,
And prays in untold sorrow at last to win
To a long-lost Paradise an entering-in.
O yearning eyes that through earth's ages scan
The " glorious misery " 'tis to be a man;
Secure in quiet arms that Saviour be,
Whose name is Innocency.

DIVINE DELIGHT

Dark, dark this mind, if ever in vain it rove
The face of man in search of hope and love;
Or, turning inward from earth's sun and moon,
Spin in cold solitude thought's mazed cocoon
Fresh hang Time's branches. Hollow in space out-cry.
The grave-toned trumpets of Eternity.
" World of divine delight," heart whispereth,
Though all its all lie but 'twixt birth and death.

ENVOY

Child, do you love the flower
Shining with colour and dew
Lighting its transient hour?
So I love you.

[293]

The lambs in the mead are at play,
'Neath a hurdle the shepherd's asleep,
From height to height of the day
　　The sunbeams sweep.

Evening will come. And alone
The dreamer the dark will beguile;
All the world will be gone
　　For a dream's brief while.

Then I shall be old; and away:
And you, with sad joy in your eyes,
Will brood over children at play
　　With as loveful surmise.

THE SONG OF THE SECRET

Where is beauty?
　Gone, gone:
The cold winds have taken it
　With their faint moan;
The white stars have shaken it,
　Trembling down,
Into the pathless deeps of the sea:
　Gone, gone
Is beauty from me.

The clear naked flower
　Is faded and dead;
The green-leafed willow,
　Drooping her head,
Whispers low to the shade
　Of her boughs in the stream,
Sighing a beauty
Secret as dream.

THE SONG OF SEVEN

Far away, and long ago —
May sweet Memory be forgiven!
Came a Wizard in the evening,
And he sang the Song of Seven.
Yes, he plucked his jangling harp-strings
With fingers smooth and even;
And his eyes beneath his dangling hair
Were still as is the sea;
But the Song of Seven has never yet,
One note, come back to me.

The Song of One I know,
A rose its thorns between;

The Song of Two I learned
Where only the birds have been;

The Song of Three I heard
When March was fleet with hares;

The Song of Four was the wind's — the wind's,
Where wheat grew thick with tares;

[295]

The Song of Five, ah me!
Lovely the midmost one;

The Song of Six, died out
Before the dream was done. . . .

One — two — three — four — five, six —
And all the grace notes given:
But *widdershins,* and witchery-sweet,
Where is the Song of Seven?

UNDER THE ROSE

(*The Song of the Wanderer*)

Nobody, nobody told me
What nobody, nobody knows:
But now I know where the Rainbow ends,
I know where there grows
A Tree that's called the Tree of Life,
I know where there flows
The River of All-Forgottenness,
And where the Lotus blows,
And I — I've trodden the forest, where
In flames of gold and rose,
To burn, and then arise again,
    The Phoenix goes.

Nobody, nobody told me
What nobody, nobody knows;
Hide thy face in a veil of light,
Put on thy silver shoes,
Thou art the Stranger I know best,
Thou are the sweetheart, who
Came from the Land between Wake and Dream,
Cold with the morning dew.

SOMEWHERE

Would you tell me the way to Somewhere?
  Somewhere, *Somewhere,*
  I have heard of a place called Somewhere —
  But know not where it can be.
      It makes no difference,
      Whether or not
      I go in dreams
      Or trudge on foot:
Could you tell me the way to Somewhere,
  The Somewhere meant for me?

There's a little old house in Somewhere —
  *Some*where, *Some*where,
A queer little house, with a Cat and a Mouse —
  Just room enough for three.
      A kitchen, a larder,
      A bin for bread,
      A string of candles,
      Or stars instead,
      A table, a chair,
      And a four-post bed —
There's room for us all in Somewhere,
  For the Cat and the Mouse and Me.

Puss is called *Skimme* in Somewhere,
  In *Some*where, *Some*where;
Miaou, miaou, in Somewhere,
  S — K — I — M — M — E.
      Miss Mouse is scarcely
      One inch tall,
      So *she* never needed
      A name at all;
      And though you call,
      And call, and call,
      There squeaks no answer,
      Great or small —

Though her tail is a sight times longer
  Than this is likely to be: —
          FOR
I want to be *off* to Somewhere,
To far, lone, lovely Somewhere,
No matter where Somewhere be.

        It makes no difference
        Whether or not
        I flit in sleep
        Or trudge on foot,
        Or this time tomorrow
        How far I've got,
        Summer or Winter,
        Cold, or hot,
        Where, or When,
        Or Why, or What —
Please, tell me the way to Somewhere —
        *Some*where, *Some*where;
Somewhere, *Some*where, *Somewhere,* SOMEWHERE —
  The Somewhere meant for me!

THE JOURNEY

    When the high road
    Forks into a by-road,
    And this leads down
    To a lane,
    And the lane fades into
    A bridle-path,
    Green with the long night's rain,
    Through a forest winding up and on —
    Moss, fern, and sun-bleached bone —
    Till hardly a trace
    Remains;

And this thins out
Into open wild,
High under heaven,
With sunset filled,
A bluff of cliff,
Wide, trackless, wild;
And a path is sought
In vain. . . .

It is then that the Ocean
May heave into sight,
A gulf enringed
With a burning white,
A sea of darkness,
Dazzling bright;
And Islands — peaks
Of such beauty that
A secret danger lies in wait,
And soul and sense are afraid thereat;
And an Ariel music
On the breeze
Thrills the mind
With a lorn unease;
And every thorn, and bird, and flower,
And every time-worn stone
A challenge cries on the trespasser,
Beware! Thou art alone! . . .

It is then that the air
Breathes strangely sweet,
And the heart within
Can scarcely beat,
Since the Journey
Is just begun:
The Journey
Is nearly done.

"I DREAM OF A PLACE"

I dream of a place where I long to live always:
Green hills, shallow sand dunes, and nearing the sea;

The house is of stone; there are twelve lattice windows,
And a door, with a keyhole — though lost is the key.

Thick-thatched is the roof; it has low, white-washed chimneys,
Where doves preen their wings, and coo, *Please,* love; love *me!*

There martins are flitting; the sun shines; the moon shines;
Drifts of bright flowers are adrone with the bee;

And a wonderful music of bird-song at daybreak
Wells up from the bosom of every tree.

A brook of clear water encircles the garden,
With kingcups, and cress, and the white *fleur de lys* —

Moorhens and dabchicks; the wild duck at evening
Wing away to the sun, in the shape of a V;

And the night shows the stars, shining in at the windows
Brings nearer the far-away sigh of the sea.

Oh, the quiet, the green of the grass, the grey willows,
The light, and the shine, and the air sweet and free! —

That dream of a place where I long to live always:
Low hills, shallow sand dunes — at peace there to be!

KNOWN OF OLD

" I dream, and I dream. . . ."

" Speak! what do you dream? "

" That I see Phantoms walking,
Translucent as flame,
In a place, known of old,
Though now lost is its name —
A place of a peace
So profound that I seem
As serenely at rest
As a leaf on a stream. —
I dream, and I dream. . . .

" Yet no strangers are these
Who in ecstasy stray
Where the moon high in heaven,
Shines open as day.

" Their robes are of light,
And each calm solemn face,
In the crystalline night,
Of grief shows no trace,
But shines with the joy
Of an infinite grace.
So, with gladness I weep,
As in rapture and silence,
Aloof, and yet near me,
They move in my sleep;
And their voices repeat
Words ancient and sweet —
A rune once I knew,
But, alas, now forget,
A rune known of old
Which, alas, I forget. —
I dream, and I dream . . .

" And that is my dream."

GONE

Where's the Queen of Sheba?
Where King Solomon?
Gone with Boy Blue who looks after the sheep,
Gone and gone and gone.

Lovely is the sunshine;
Lovely is the wheat;
Lovely the wind from out of the clouds
Having its way with it.

Rise up, Old Green-Stalks!
Delve deep, Old Corn!
But where's the Queen of Sheba?
Where King Solomon?

THE SONG OF SHADOWS

Sweep thy faint strings, Musician,
    With thy long lean hand;
Downward the starry tapers burn,
    Sinks soft the waning sand;
The old hound whimpers couched in sleep,
    The embers smoulder low;
Across the walls the shadows
    Come, and go.

Sweep softly thy strings, Musician,
    The minutes mount to hours;
Frost on the windless casement weaves
    A labyrinth of flowers;
Ghosts linger in the darkening air,
    Hearken at the open door;
Music hath called them, dreaming,
    Home once more.

THE SONG OF THE MAD PRINCE

Who said, " Peacock Pie " ?
    The old King to the sparrow:
Who said, " Crops are ripe " ?
    Rust to the harrow:
Who said, " Where sleeps she now ?
    Where rests she now her head,
Bathed in eve's loveliness ? " —
    That's what I said.

Who said, " Ay, mum's the word ";
    Sexton to willow:
Who said, " Green dusk for dreams,
    Moss for a pillow " ?
Who said, " All Time's delight
    Hath she for narrow bed;
Life's troubled bubble broken " ? —
    That's what I said.

A Child's
Day

I

I sang a song to Rosamond Rose
Only the wind in the twilight knows:
I sang a song to Jeanetta Jennie,
She flung from her window a silver penny:
I sang a song to Matilda May,
She took to her heels and ran away:
I sang a song to Susannah Sue,
She giggled the whole of the verses through:

But nevertheless, as sweet as I can,
I'll sing a song to Elizabeth Ann —
The same little Ann as there you see
Smiling as happy as happy can be.
And all that my song is meant to say
Is just what she did one long, long day,
With her own little self to play with only,
Yet never once felt the least bit lonely.

II

Softly, drowsily,
Out of sleep;
Into the world again
Ann's eyes peep;
Over the pictures
Across the walls
One little quivering
Sunbeam falls.
A thrush in the garden
Seems to say,
Wake, little Ann,

'Tis day, 'tis day!
Faint sweet breezes
The casement stir,
Breathing of pinks
And lavender.
At last from her pillow,
With cheeks bright red,
Up comes her round little
Tousled head;
And out she tumbles
From her warm bed.

III

Little birds bathe
In the sunny dust.
Whether they want to,
Or not, they *must*.
Seal and Walrus
And Polar Bear
One green icy
Wash-tub share.
Alligator,
Nor Hippopot-
Amus ever
His bath forgot.
Out of his forest
The Elephant tramps
To squirt himself
In his gloomy swamps.
On crackling fins
From the deep sea fly
Flying-fish into
The air to dry.
Silver Swans
In shallows green
Their dew-bespangled
Pinions preen.
And all day long
Wash Duck and Drake
In their duckweed pond —
For washing's sake.
So, in her lonesome,
Slippety, bare,
Elizabeth Ann's
Splash — splashing there;
And now from the watery
Waves amonje
Stands slooshing herself
With that 'normous sponge.

Puma, Panther, Leopard, and Lion
Nothing but green grass have to dry on,
Seals and Walruses in a trice
Flick their water-drops into Ice;

Back to his forests the Elephant swings
Caked in mud against bites and stings;
As for the plump Hippopotamus,
He steams himself dry to save a fuss;
And the bird that cries to her mate Quack, Quack!
Is oily by nature if not by knack,
So the water pearls off *her* beautiful back.

But sailing the world's wide ocean round,
In a big broad bale from Turkey bound,
All for the sake of Elizabeth Ann
This towel's been sent by a Mussulman,
And with might and main she must rub — rub — rub —
Till she's warm and dry from her morning tub.

IV

The Queen of Arabia, Uanjinee,
Slaves to dress her had thirty-three;
Eleven in scarlet, eleven in rose,
Eleven in orange, as every one knows;
And never was lady lovelier than she —
The Queen of Arabia, Uanjinee.

Yet — though, of course, 'twould be vain to tell a-
Nother word about Cinderella —
Except for a Mouse on the chimney shelf,
She put on her slippers quite — quite by herself,
And I can't help thinking the greater pleasure
Is to dress in haste, and look lovely at leisure.
Certainly summer or winter, Ann
Always dresses as quick as she can.

[309]

V

England over,
And all June through,
Daybreak's peeping
At half-past two.
Roses and dewdrops
Begin to be
Wonderful lovely
At half-past three.
Gulls and cormorants
On the shore
Squabble for fishes
At half-past four.
The great Queen Bee
In her golden hive
Is sleek with nectar
By half-past five.

The ravening birds
In the farmer's ricks
Are hungry for luncheon
At half-past six.
While all the pigs
From York to Devon
Have finished their wash
Before half-past seven.
But Elizabeth Ann
Gets up so late
She has only begun
At half-past eight
To gobble her porridge up —
Hungry soul —
Tucked up in a bib,
Before her bowl.

VI

Thousands of years ago,
    In good King George's isles,
Forest — to forest — to forest spread,
    For miles and miles and miles.
All kinds of beasts roamed there,
    Drank of Teviot and Thames,
Beasts of all shapes and sizes and colors,
    But without any names.
And snug and shag in his coat,
    With green little eyes aglare,
Trod on his paws, with tapping of claws,
    The beast men now call Bear;
Lurched on his legs and stole
    Out of the rifts in the trees
All the sweet oozy summer-sun comb
    Of the poor little bees;
Sat in the glades and caught
    Flies by the hour,
Munched 'em up, just like a dog,
    Sweet with the sour.
But Time, she nods her head —
    Like flights of the butterfly,
Mammoths fade through her hours;
    And Man draws nigh.
And it's ages and ages ago;
    Felled are the forests, in ruin;
Gone are the thickets where lived on his lone Old Bruin.

VII

When safe into the fields Ann got,
She chose a dappled, shady spot,
Beside a green, rush-bordered pool,
Where, over water still and cool,

The little twittering birds did pass,
Like shadows in a looking-glass.
Ann slily looked this way, and that;
And then took off her shady hat.
She peeped — and peeped; off came her frock,
Followed in haste by shoe and sock.
Then softly, slowly, down she went
To where the scented rushes bent,
And all among the fishes put
Like a great giant, her little foot,
And paddled slowly to and fro
Each little tiny thirsty toe.
Then dabbling in the weeds she drew
Her fingers the still water through,
Trying in vain with groping hand
To coax a stickleback to land;
But when she had nearly housed him in,
Away he'd dart on flickering fin,
The softly wavering stalks between.

VIII

When she was in her garden,
And playing with her ball,
Ann heard a distant music
On the other side of the wall —
A far-off singing, shrill and sweet,
In the still and sunshine day,
And these the words were of the song
That voice did sing and say: —

" Happy, happy it is to be
Where the greenwood hangs o'er the dark blue sea;
To roam in the moonbeams clear and still
And dance with the elves
Over dale and hill;

To taste their cups, and with them roam
The fields for dewdrops and honeycomb.
Climb then, and come, as quick as you can,
And dwell with the fairies, Elizabeth Ann! "

Ann held her ball, and listened;
The faint song died away;
And it seemed it was a dream she'd dreamed
In the hot and sunshine day;
She heard the whistling of the birds,
The droning of the bees;
And then once more the singing came,
And now the words were these: —

" Never, never, comes tear or sorrow,
In the mansions old where the fairies dwell;
But only the harping of their sweet harp-strings,
And the lonesome stroke of a distant bell,
Where upon hills of thyme and heather,
The shepherd sits with his wandering sheep;
And the curlew wails, and the skylark hovers
Over the sand where the conies creep;
Climb then, and come, as quick as you can,
And dwell with the fairies, Elizabeth Ann! "

And just as Ann a-tiptoe crept,
Under the old green wall,
To where a stooping cherry tree
Grew shadowy and tall;
Above the fairy's singing
Hollow and shrill and sweet,
That seemed to make her heart stand still,
And then more wildly beat,
Came Susan's voice a-calling " Ann!
Come quick as you are able;
And wash your grubby hands, my dear,
For dinner's on the table! "

There was an old woman who lived in the Fens
Who had for her breakfast two nice fat hens.

There was an old woman who lived at Licke
Whatever she gobbled up gobbled up quick.

There was an old woman who lived at Bow
Who waited until her guests should go.

There was an old woman who lived at Ware
Supped on red-currant jelly and cold jugged hare.

There was an old woman who lived at Bury
Who always ate in a violent hurry.

There was an old woman who lived at Flint
Fed her sheep on parsley, her lambs on mint.

There was an old woman who lived at Cork
Lunched with her nevvy on peas and pork.

There was an old woman who lived at Greenwich
Went out with a candle to cut herself spinach.

There was an old woman who lived at Hull
Who never stopped eating till she was full.

There was an old woman who lived at Diss
Who couldn't abide greens, gristle, or grease.

There was an old woman who lived at Thame
Who ate up the courses just as they came.

There was an old woman who lived at Tring
At meals did nothing but laugh and sing.

There was an old woman who lived at Steep
Who still munched on though fast asleep.

There was an old woman who lived at Wick
Whose teeth did nothing but clash and click.

There was an old woman who lived at Lundy
Always had hash for dinner on Monday.

There was an old woman who lived at Dover
Threw to her pigs whatever was over.

X

This little morsel of morsels here —
Just what it is is not quite clear:
It might be pudding, it might be meat,
Cold, or hot, or salt, or sweet;
Baked, or roasted, or broiled, or fried;
Bare, or frittered, or puddinged, or pied;
Cooked in a saucepan, jar, or pan —
But it's all the same to Elizabeth Ann.
For when one's hungry it doesn't much matter
So long as there's *something* on one's platter.

XI

Now fie! O fie! How sly a face!
Half greedy joy, and half disgrace;
O foolish Ann, O greedy finger,
To long for that forbidden ginger!

O Ann, the story I could tell! —
What horrid, horrid things befell

Two gluttonous boys who soft did creep,
While Cook was in her chair asleep,
Into a cupboard, there to make
A feast on stolen tipsy-cake —
Which over night they had hid themselves,
On one of her store cupboard shelves;
They ate so much, they ate so fast,
They both were sadly stuffed at last.
Drowsy and stupid, blowsed and blown,
In sluggish sleep they laid them down,
And soon rose up a stifled snore
From where they huddled on the floor.
And, presently, Cook, passing by,
Her cupboard door ajar did spy,
And that all safe her stores might be,
Turned with her thumb the noiseless key.
Night came with blackest fears to wrack
Those greedy knaves (named Dick and Jack).
They woke; and in the stuffy gloom
Waited in vain for Cook to come.
They dared not knock, or kick, or shout,
Not knowing *who* might be about.
The days dragged on. Their parents said,
" Poor Dick and Jack; they must be dead! "
Hungrier and hungrier they grew;
They searched the darksome cupboard through;
Candles, and soda, salt, and string,
Soap, glue — they ate up everything:
Nothing but shadows they seemed to be,
Gnawing a stick of wood for tea.
At length, at last, alas! alack!
Jack looked at Dick; and Dick at Jack;
And in his woe each famished brother
Turned in the dusk and ate the other.

So when Cook came to open the door,
Nothing was there upon the floor;
As with her candle she stood there,

Ceiling to floor the place was bare;
Not even a little heap of bones
That had been two fat brothers once!

And see! That foolish Ann's forgot
To put the cover on the pot;
And also smeared — the heedless ninny —
Her sticky fingers on her pinny.
And, O dear me! without a doubt,
Mamma has found the culprit out.
And Ann is weeping many a tear;
And shame has turned her back, poor dear;
Lonely and angry, in disgrace,
She's hiding her poor mottled face.
But ginger now will tempt in vain;
She'll never, never taste again.

XII

Ann, upon the stroke of three,
Halfway 'twixt dinner-time and tea,
Cosily tucked in her four-legged chair,
With nice clean hands and smooth brushed hair,
In some small secret nursery nook,
Sits with her big Picture-book.

There Puss in Boots, with sidelong eye
And bushy tail goes mincing by;

Peering into an empty cupboard
With her old Dog stoops Mother Hubbard;

Beside a bushy bright-green Wood
Walks with the Wolf Red Ridinghood;

In their small cottage the Three Bears,
Each at his bowl of Porridge stares;

There's striking Clock — and scampering Mouse;
The King of Hearts' cool Counting-house;

There a Fine Lady rides all day,
But never, never rides away;

While Jack and Jill for ever roll;
And drinks to his Fiddlers Old King Cole

And though Ann's little busy head
Can't quite get down from A to Z,
She is content to sit and look
At her bright-colored Picture-book.

XIII

As soon as ever twilight comes,
    Ann creeps upstairs to pass,
With one tall candle, just an hour
    Before her looking-glass.
She rummages old wardrobes in,
    Turns dusty boxes out;
And nods and curtseys, dances, sings,
    And hops and skips about.
Her candle's lean long yellow beam
    Shines softly in the gloom,
And through the window's gathering night
    Stars peep into the room.

Ages and ages and ages ago,
Ann's great-grandmother dressed just so;
In a big poke-bonnet, a Paisley shawl,
Climbed into her coach to make a call;
And over the cobble-stones jogged away,
To drink with her daughter a dish of tay.
Then nice little boys wore nankeen breeches;
And demure little girls with fine silk stitches
Learned to make samplers of beasts and birds
And ever so many most difficult words.
Then Anns and Matildas and Sams and Dicks
Were snoring in blankets long before six.
And every night with a tallow candle,
And a warming-pan with a four-foot handle,
The maids came up to warm the bed
(And burnt a great hole in the sheet instead).
Then pretty maids blushed, and said, " My nines! "
At hundreds of thousands of Valentines.
Then never came May but danced between
Robin and Marion, Jack-in-the-Green;
Then saged and onioned, and stewed in its juice,
To table on Michaelmas Day sailed Goose;
Gunpowder Treason and Plot to remember,

Bonfires blazed on the fifth of November;
And never the Waits did a-carolling go
In less than at least a yard of snow.

So — poor little Ann a sigh must smother
Because she isn't her great-grandmother.

XIV

Now, dear me!
What's this we see?
A dreadful G —
H — O — S — T!
A-glowering with
A chalk-white face

Out of some dim
And dismal place.
Oh, won't poor Nurse
Squeal out, when she
Comes up, that dreadful
Shape to see!

She'll pant and say,
" O la! Miss Ann,
I thought you was
A bogey-man!
Now! look at them
Untidy clo'es!
And, did you ever,
What a nose!
If you was in
A smock, Miss Ann,
They'd take you for
The Miller's man.
To see the mischief
You have done,
And me not twenty minutes gone! "

XV

" Now, my dear, for gracious sake,
Eat up this slice of currant cake;
Though, certain sure, you'll soon be screaming
For me to come — and find you dreaming.
In *my* young days in bed we'd be
Once we had swallowed down our tea.
And cake! — we'd dance if mother spread
A scrap of butter on our bread!
Except my brother, little Jack,
Who was, poor mite, a humptyback.
But there! times change; he's grown a man;
And I'm no chick myself, Miss Ann.
Now, don't 'ee move a step from here,
I shan't be gone for long, my dear! "

But soon as Nurse's back was turned
Ann's idle thumbs for mischief yearned.
See now, those horrid scissors, oh,

If they should slip an inch or so!
If Ann should jog or jerk — suppose
They snipped off her small powdery nose!
If she should sneeze, or cough, or laugh,
They might divide her quite in half;
They might this best of little daughters
Slice into four quite equal quaughters.
And though she plagues her nurse, poor soul,
She'd much prefer Miss Mischief whole,
Would wring her hands in sad distraction
O'er each belov'd but naughty fraction.

This then had been our last, last rhyme,
Had Nurse not just returned in time.
For when Ann heard her on the stairs
She hid in haste those wicked shears;
And there as meek as " Little Jimmie "
Was seated smiling in her shimmie.

XVI

The King in slumber when he lies down
Hangs up in a cupboard his golden crown;
The Lord High Chancellor snores in peace
Out of his Garter and Golden Fleece;
No Plenipotentiary lays him flat
Till he's dangled on bedpost his gold Cockhat;
And never to attic has Page-boy mounted
Before his forty-four buttons are counted;

But higgledy-piggledy
Slovenly Ann
Jumps out of her clothes
As fast as she can;
And with frock, sock, shoe
Flung anywhere,

Slips from dressdupedness
Into her bare.
Now, just as when the day began,
Without one clo', sits little Ann,
A-toasting in this scant attire
Her cheeks before the nursery fire.

Golden palaces there she sees,
With fiery fountains, flaming trees;
Through darkling arch and smouldering glen
March hosts of little shimmering men,
To where beneath the burning skies
A blazing salamander lies,
Breathing out sparks and smoke the while
He watches them with hungry smile.

XVII

Now, through the dusk
With muffled bell
The Dustman comes
The world to tell,
Night's elfin lanterns
Burn and gleam
In the twilight, wonderful
World of Dream.

Hollow and dim
Sleep's boat doth ride,
Heavily still
At the waterside.
Patter, patter,
The children come,
Yawning and sleepy,
Out of the gloom.

Like droning bees
In a garden green,
Over the thwarts
They clamber in.
And lovely Sleep
With long-drawn oar
Turns away
From the whispering shore.

Over the water
Like roses glide
Her hundreds of passengers
Packed inside,
To where in her garden
Tremble and gleam
The harps and lamps
Of the World of Dream.

XVIII

He squats by the fire
    On his three-legged stool,
When all in the house
    With slumber are full.

And he warms his great hands,
    Hanging loose from each knee.
And he whistles as soft
    As the night-wind at sea.

For his work now is done;
    All the water is sweet;
He has turned each brown loaf,
    And breathed magic on it.

The milk in the pan,
    And the bacon on beam
He has " spelled " with his thumb,
    And bewitched has the dream.

Not a mouse, not a moth,
    Not a spider but sat,
And quaked as it wondered
    What next he'd be at.

But his heart, O, his heart —
    It belies his great nose;
And at gleam of his eye
    Not a soul would suppose

He had stooped with great thumbs,
    And big thatched head,
To tuck his small mistress
    More snugly in bed.

Who would think, now, a throat
So lank and so thin
Might make birds seem to warble
In the dream she is in!

Now hunched by the fire,
While the embers burn low,
He nods until daybreak,
And at daybreak he'll go.

Soon the first cock will 'light
From his perch and point high
His beak at the Ploughboy
Grown pale in the sky;

And crow will he shrill;
Then, meek as a mouse,
Lob will rouse up and shuffle
Straight out of the house.

His supper for breakfast;
For wages his work;
And to warm his great hands
Just an hour in the mirk.

XIX

Sadly, O, sadly, the sweet bells of Baddeley
Played in their steeples when Robin was gone,
Killed by an arrow,
Shot by Cock Sparrow,
Out of a Maybush, fragrant and wan.

Grievedly, grievedly, tolled distant Shieveley,
When the Dwarfs laid poor Snow-White asleep on the hill
Drowsed by an apple,
The Queen, sly and subtle,
Had cut with her knife on the blossomy sill.

XX

This brief day now over;
Life's but a span.
Tell how my heart aches,
Tell how my heart breaks,
To bid now farewell
To Elizabeth Ann.

Lullay O, lullaby,
Sing this sad roundelay,
Muted the strings;
Since Sorrow began,
The World's said goodbye, Ann,
And so too, must I, Ann;
Child of one brief day,
Elizabeth Ann.

FIRST LINE INDEX

[327]

[328]

[333]

[337]

TITLE INDEX

[339]